T0146911

Elevated BY
EXPERIENCES

Elevated BY EXPERIENCES

A Spiritual Guide to Help Women Overcome Past
Adversity and Create an Intentional, Authentic Life

Dr. Keke M. Robinson

ELEVATED BY EXPERIENCES
A SPIRITUAL GUIDE TO HELP WOMEN
OVERCOME PAST ADVERSITY AND CREATE
AN INTENTIONAL, AUTHENTIC LIFE

iUniverse books may be ordered through booksellers or by contacting:

iUniverse
1663 Liberty Drive
Bloomington, IN 47403
www.iuniverse.com
1-800-Authors (1-800-288-4677)

ISBN: 978-1-5320-2653-9 (sc)
ISBN: 978-1-5320-2652-2 (e)

Library of Congress Control Number: 2017913493

Print information available on the last page.

iUniverse rev. date: 12/07/2017

CONTENTS

DEDICATION

Kiera, Tia, Akilia, and Stedmon:
I am so proud and grateful that you are creating your
own experiences, but most importantly, that you are being
elevated by God's love, grace, favor, and mercy...

ACKNOWLEDGEMENT

I would like to acknowledge and sincerely thank my father, Wallace Guidry, for his constant belief in me. His support and reassurance have been the very foundation of my life. His character, integrity, strength, kindness, candor, and generosity has been unwavering.

He embodies characteristics that are worthy to be emulated. He has always encouraged me to pursue my goals. His genuineness is truly profound and heartfelt; I am eternally grateful.

Whenever my self-doubt would emerge, he would gently remind me of my gifts and reiterate his poignant phrase that undeniably repositioned me to: believe in myself; remain faithful to my vision; become a fearless change agent; soar in my purpose; acknowledge my skills and talents; have confidence in knowing that I literally possess the fundamental keys to my own success.

His unconditional love is a continuous reminder that my mistakes have no power and my dreams have no limits.

You are not going to starve... ~ Mr. Wallace Guidry

DEFINITIONS

Elevate *(verb). (1) Raise or lift to a higher position. (2) Raise to a more important or impressive level.*

Synonyms: *promote, upgrade, advance*
(Webster Dictionary)

Experiences *(noun). Practical contact with and observation of facts or events.*

Synonyms: *involvement in, participation in, contact with, acquaintance with, exposure to, observation of, awareness of, insight into*
(Webster Dictionary)

OVERVIEW

Elevated by Experiences is an interactive book and workbook that includes affirmations, biblical scriptures, and self-coaching questions.

It is an easy-read, comprised of five chapters that are a compilation of inspiring stories composed to motivate you to overcome past mistakes, live the highest expression of your best self, express gratitude, create boundaries, follow your dreams, and *set the intention to create an authentic life.*

After each chapter, you will find self-coaching questions that you can answer as you read or ponder your responses for later. There is also a section included for you to chronicle reflective notes about what resonated with you. I would suggest that you review your responses and notes, periodically, to gauge your personal growth.

A Brief Snippet About Each Chapter:

Chapter I: *Elevated by Pain and Past Mistakes-* Focuses on how to break free from your past and transform your pain into an empowering platform that will fulfill your purpose. Transition and utilize what was meant to break you into a powerful resource of strength and wisdom that will become a blessing to you and others.

Chapter II: *Elevated by Being Balanced-* Explores how to form a harmonious life balance to ensure that you are receiving as much as you are giving. Analyze the importance of creating necessary boundaries. Evaluate how to validate that you are making yourself a priority in your own life. It is essential that you develop the courage to release anyone or anything that is not in alignment with your purpose.

Chapter III: *Elevated by Faith and Gratitude-* Delves into the benefits of evoking your faith to strengthen your spiritual walk. Always remember to believe in yourself, despite how dire your current situation may appear. When you are grateful for what you have, you invite more possibilities into your life. You will become opened to receive more and to become more.

Chapter IV: *Elevated by Empowerment-* Learn how the word "No" can be liberating, beneficial, and empowering. Explore the concept of how changing your thoughts can change your life. Recognize that you have the power to create the type of life that you desire and deserve. Do not be afraid to fail; no risk, no reward. You will never know what you could truly become if you don't try. Take a leap of faith; catapult into your calling. The world is waiting for your gift.

Chapter V: *Elevated by Being Authentic-* Assess your authenticity. It is so imperative that you set the intention to create an authentic life. Discovering your true identity affords you an opportunity to manifest wisdom, self-love, self-acceptance, power, freedom of choice, and genuine happiness. God created you to be amazing. Never dim your light for anyone. BE unapologetically authentic.

It is good for me that I have been afflicted; that
I might learn thy statues. ~ Psalm 119:71

PREFACE

Grappling with the struggle to discover my true identity has led to a plethora of wrong choices, indecisiveness, discontentment, low self-worth, and monumental pain. Often feeling like a stranger within my own body, I never believed that I truly belonged anywhere. My environments were never, ever quite consistently *right*. I was *with* the crowd, but I was never *of* the crowd. I *knew* that I was out-of-place. At times, the loneliness that I felt became indescribable. I would often seek peace, happiness, or self-fulfillment elsewhere; I failed to realize that anything that I ever needed or wanted was already *within* me. *I* was what I had been searching for. *(Note: I am the master of my fate. I am the captain of my soul. ~ William Ernest Henley)*

As a young girl and into my early adulthood, I was in limbo. I found myself languishing betwixt and between prominent stages. I did not fit where I was but I wasn't yet prepared or qualified for where I wanted to go. The strife I would encounter would reap havoc on my psyche and the confusion would be amplified because I couldn't understand why certain situations were 'happening to me.' I had not, yet, gleaned the notion that I had the power to create the type of life that I wanted; that I was in charge of designing my destiny.

When I gradually began to gain a sense of self-awareness and confidence, it was suggested that I stifle my voice. It was duly-noted that having a voice is a direct act of leadership. My self-expression was deemed intimidating, so I couldn't truly be myself because it may offend others. *(Note: When a girl tries to lead, she is often labeled bossy. ~ Sheryl Sandberg)* It was recommended that I be more subdued; become less bold, vocal, or strong. Be less domineering and direct; become more docile or coy because some individuals couldn't handle bruised egos. This type of gullible, submissive behavior would be rewarded or promoted. I would *'play along, to get along.'* This imposter façade only made me more miserable.

After being stagnant for so long, I yearned for self-growth and enlightenment. I had this gnawing inside of me that would not go away. I was rapidly outgrowing certain individuals and environments. I rejected the notion of settling for 'just good enough'; it was *not* good enough. I knew I was made for much more. I embarked on my quest to discover God's purpose for my life. It was this mental shift that ultimately, changed the course of my life. Once, I began to seek God, I began to find myself. My spiritual awakening placed me on the path towards my destiny. I evolved into being unapologetically authentic.

Through mindfulness, prayer and meditation, I began to recognize that those stressful situations were the works of God's hand ensuring that I did not become too comfortable and complacent at a particular level. A hater's role was to serve as confirmation that I possessed great potential and that those current situations were not my final destination. Life's tests were road maps providing strategic directions for my self-discovery journey. There is no such thing as failure if I could ascertain something valuable in the process.

Just because one scene did not go according to plan, it does not equate to the culminating basis of my entire life story. I was reminded to never make a permanent decision regarding a temporary situation. It will change, and I will adapt accordingly. I am the author of my story. I do not need to put a period where there only needs to be a comma or semicolon. I can turn the page to begin a new chapter. I can pause and insert *"To Be Continued..."*, if necessary. My narrative doesn't have to be written perfectly because I have the best editor in the world, God, and He will proofread my life's manuscript and correct any errors to my storyline.

I had to evoke the *gift of goodbye* to release some things and people from my life. By auditing my inner circle, I strategically removed any perceived toxicity out of my environment. If it did not align with my vision or destiny, it was detrimental to my growth. Surrounding myself with like-minded people, helped me to realize that I wasn't intimidating or demanding. These associations exposed me to an array of confident, successful, passionate influencers that I admired for their perseverance, hard work, and tenacity. People that know what they want, where they are going, and have devised a plan of action to execute are purpose-driven individuals.

Possessing a vision for my future did not make me menacing; it made me intentional. A made-up mind is very powerful. I had to make myself a priority in my own life. I refuse to dim my light, to placate others' insecurities. It is essential to shine the brightest during the darkest of times. I do not have to feel guilty about my accomplishments or my failures nor do I need others' validation or endorsement. I do not have to censor myself. I garnered that when I stand in my truth, I stand in my power. With God, all things are possible and I would be doing myself a disservice by settling for anything less than I deserve. I embraced my authentic self and became committed to operating in my calling.

Yes, I have made some regrettable mistakes, and I take full ownership of my errs. I would change it if I could, but I cannot. But, what I can do is make peace with my past and refuse to be held hostage by it any longer. Regardless of what I had been through, I made the decision to set the intention to begin anew. Learning from my mistakes has assisted me with cultivating wisdom and developing my character. *(Note: Mistakes are a fact of life. It is the response to the error that counts. ~ Nikki Giovanni)* Initially, it was challenging to change my thinking. But, once I pivoted my position, my new positive outlook began to yield productive outcomes.

My pain became my platform to encourage, educate, equip, and empower others. My past no longer defines me, instead it has made me better. Many misfortunes occurred because of my choices and some trials came because of others' actions. Nevertheless, it was up to me how I would respond to those mishaps. Much of my plight wasn't even about me; it was predestined so that God could get the glory. *It was in my brokenness that I found my blessing.* My pain birthed my purpose. My transformation is my testimony that if God can do it for me, He can do it for you.

Transitioning from being a statistical teenage mother to obtaining a doctoral degree, in Educational Leadership, was no small feat. By getting myself together, I have seen the positive ripple effects transpire in every area of my life. In my immediate family, I have witnessed generational curses being broken one by one. I am keenly aware that my circumstances could have been completely different.

As an educator, speaker, certified life coach, an authenticity researcher, and a woman that has endured an influx of pain and past mistakes, I am dedicated to inspiring others, particularly young girls and women, to exemplify authenticity, strive for greatness, and to live the highest expression of their best selves. Do not be afraid to ask for what you want. This is not a dress rehearsal. We only get one shot at this life, so you may as well be who you truly are. There is no need to worry about yesterday. It happened; it is over. Focus on creating a better tomorrow.

I worked for menial's hire, only to learned dismayed.
That any wage I had asked of Life, Life would
have willingly paid. ~ Jessie B. Rittenhouse

Shedding the layers and getting to my core has been the most fear-provoking, unsettling, probing, enlightening, joyous, rewarding charge that I have been entrusted with. I belong to God and I am responsible for this precious temple that He has gifted me. I am learning to take care of myself and that begins with a sound mind, clean heart, pure intentions, and a commitment to fulfilling my divinely-assigned calling.

Each day, I am humbled and so grateful for the Lord's forgiveness and His 2nd, 3rd, 4th, 5th, … 11th, *etc.* chances. I have literally witnessed His grace and protection shield me from the enemy's attacks. I walked away unscathed from a potentially fatal vehicle accident. Without a doubt, I know that God's angels have a protective hedge around me. I do not want to get to the end of my life and have not fulfilled the meaningful purpose of why God created me. I have an obligation to walk in my destiny and to create my legacy. *It is my prayer and my mission to help you to do the same…*

A spiritual gift is given to each of us so we can
help each other. ~ 1 Corinthians 12:7-11

INTRODUCTION

*But until a person can say deeply and honestly, "I am what
I am today because of the choices I made yesterday," that
person cannot say, "I choose otherwise." ~ Stephen Covey*

Many of us have faced ordeals in our lives that we were certain would cause our downfall. The unsuccessful encounters can manipulate how we feel about ourselves and the negative experiences can lead to what may be perceived as extreme setbacks. Here is an important takeaway: *You do not have to allow your past relationships or circumstances to inhibit your growth.*

You can pivot those *setbacks* into *setups* to build a strong foundation for your *comeback*. You can reemerge stronger and better than ever before. It is genuinely all about your perspective. When you are in the throes of your situation, it is hard to see the light at the end of the tunnel. You just want the pain to stop. *To stop immediately.*

Although it may hurt tremendously at the time, the pain is a midwife helping you to birth your purpose. Whatever you have endured can possibly advance you to new heights. Your past experiences have the potential to set up a new platform that will *elevate you into your destiny.*

There are numerous examples regarding individuals that became so immersed in their employment and/or titles. Once they lost that position, they were devastated. Only to later discover that they could utilize their knowledge, skills, and talents to venture into entrepreneurship and create their own successful companies.

Take into consideration when a relationship or marriage ends, some individuals had their entire identity encapsulated into their partners/ spouses. Embarking upon the journey of self-discovery to heal their broken hearts, they find a renewed sense of self-worth and they learn what to do or *not to do* in their next relationships. Gleaning from their own instructional performance manual, they become more sensitive to their needs and the needs of others. Typically, the new relationship is an upgrade and provides them with the committed and reciprocated love that they deserve.

Many of us have had hardships, heartbreaks, and/or health concerns in our lives. It may appear that the hole of despair is too deep to ever get out of, but we must remain focused on the endgame. It doesn't matter what it may look like right now, you can shift the paradigm. While you are in the midst of your storm, it may seem as though you have taken a loss, but eventually, God always seems to bless you with something or someone better.

You are the author of your 'critically acclaimed' story, so take creative control and determine how each chapter should be composed. If you do not like the format, then turn the page. It is your life; transcribe it in the way that you wish it to be read. You do not have to put a period where there only needs to be a comma or semicolon. *You can change your narrative.* If you change the story that you tell yourself, you can change your life. Do not allow yourself to become used up or defeated by your circumstances, instead, afford yourself the opportunity to become *elevated by your experiences.*

As you navigate your way through these pages, I pray that you will amass a fresh perspective regarding your past. We may not be able to control what has happened to us, but we can control (to the best of our abilities), how we respond. Certain things may not have happened *to* you, yet it may have happened *for* you. You can learn how to operate in your gifts. Make a vow to never settle for mediocrity, but instead set the standard to solely strive for excellence. You are a catalyst for change. You were made for greatness. *You are creating your legacy.*

It is my intention to ensure that you are inspired and motivated to value every personal season and recognize that the various phases are an important part of your amazing journey. Each preceding interaction is contributing to your growth. When you stand in your truth, you possess the power and courage to be your best self and to live an authentic life.

I want to encourage you to read this book multiple times with an open heart and mind to truly absorb the information. Share with your family and friends; educate others about what you have learned. Reiterate that regardless of your past, there are stories and life-changing lessons to accompany each experience. Demonstrate how you are no longer willing to be a spectator in your own life but are now determined to design your destiny.

Utilizing the coaching and reflection components of this book, analyze and evaluate your previous practices and involvements. As you reflect, journaling your responses can be very cathartic. Research has shown that it can gently guide you towards acknowledgment, self-awareness, liberating your emotions, and help to alleviate stress.

Documenting your feelings is a proven effective strategy that can yield tremendous results during your continual self-discovery journey. Be patient with yourself if you are still healing and do not have all the answers right now. Give yourself time to endure this nurturing and maturing process. But, please remember that you already possess *within* you the necessary tools and resources to cultivate your growth. *You are more than what you have been through.* **Your past does not define you, in fact, it should make you better.**

Do the best you can until you know better. Then when
you know better, do better. ~ Dr. Maya Angelou

Be Blessed,
Dr. Keke

Everything that happens is a small part of our journey. We can choose to be passive or we can be proactive and overcome our fears, set our own goals and do the best to reach them. For better or for worse, we always have a choice. ~ Giorgio Pautrie

CHAPTER 1

Elevated BY
PAIN AND PAST MISTAKES

*The best way to get rid of the pain is to feel the
pain. And when you feel the pain and go beyond
it, you'll see there's a very intense love that is
wanting to awaken itself. ~ Deepak Chopra*

Laboring Through Your Pain

Numbing the pain for a while will make it worse
when you finally feel it. ~ J.K. Rowling

When you shield the real you in fear of rejection, you create a prison within yourself. Being overly cautious when attempting to heal serves you no benefit. Do not shrink and fade into oblivion, preferring to live in a bubble because you don't want to be hurt or if you have been hurt, you are terrified of being vulnerable again. Many of us have an aversion to being hurt; pain doesn't feel good. But, you cannot cower and be courageous simultaneously.

By hiding, you do not permit yourself an opportunity to appropriately heal. You choose to live behind a mask when you do not allow your *true identity*, your *authentic* self to emerge. Shrouded in a suffocating costume, a disguise, you become content with peering within and allowing others to peek through a peephole to get a glimpse of the *real you*. Your authenticity is being obstructed; no one ever truly sees the whole picture. Although you are the main character, *the star*, you often feel reduced to being merely a cast member or an 'extra' in the production of your own life. You will continuously have that recurring inkling that you are starring in the wrong movie. You must create and follow your own script; design your destiny. If not, someone else will receive the screenwriting credit for your life.

Being reluctant to live the highest and biggest expression of your best self, causes you to lower your self-worth. When you try to find a replacement to fill a void, that you believe that you are not strong enough to face, it will never completely satisfy you. Making substitutions is not beneficial nor effective. You should not attempt to substitute pain with people, drugs, sex, food, alcohol, shopping, fast cars, risky and reckless behavior, etc. No tangible object will ever suffice; it will not work. It becomes very easy to unfairly project your pain, anger, issues or insecurities onto someone else. Generally, it can be difficult to make sound and rational decisions when you are hurting. The likely possibility is that you will, intentionally or unintentionally, hurt others.

Life doesn't get easier or more forgiving, we get stronger and more resilient. ~ Dr. Steve Maraboli

It is imperative to challenge any hidden issues and confront the pain. Camouflaging what ails you, will never reveal what could possibly restore you. It is a given that everyone at some point in their lives will face obstacles. You should not ignore the problem or attempt to run away from it. The most operative way to get over the pain is to *get over the pain.* You must deal with your circumstances and take control of your life. *Your life is your own.*

Explore the dark recesses of your mind and rebuke all negative thoughts that threaten to sabotage your self-esteem. Dodge the destructive bantering. No matter what you have been through, God can give you back your smile again. Do not permit the pain of your past to poison your endless possibilities. There is no disregarding the fact that your past did happen. Yes, it happened; it is what it is. But please remember that what's in front of you is more important than what is behind you. Everything that you have went through is making contributions and preparations for what is to come. Make peace with your past because it no longer serves where you are going. You need the closure so that you can move confidently and resiliently toward your future to begin anew. *(Note: Even if you don't receive the closure that you seek, you must continue to move forward regardless.)*

Don't quit. Suffer now and live the rest of your life as a champion. ~ Muhammad Ali

God is so proud of you. Although He already knows how your story will unfold, He monitors your progress. The notion is, 'okay if you can handle *that*, I know that you will be able to handle *this.*' The anguish that you suffer through privately, the Lord will reward you for openly.

The Lord is your strength and your portion. He will give you double for your trouble if you are faithful and stay the course. You are well-abled to get through anything. Do not continue rereading and reminiscing over previous life chapters. Write the 'bestselling' story that you were born to share with the world. Devise how the plot will materialize. Your slips or falls are not the culminating basis of your narrative. The obstinacy in your refusal to stay down is the pinnacle of your legacy. Each day is a new opportunity to grow, gain strength, and develop your character.

*If you are silent about your pain, they'll kill you
and say you enjoyed it. ~ Zora Neale Hurston*

The weapons of your warfare are not carnal. You must pray for God to bind every stronghold that attempts to come against you. If you are going to go to war and fight for yourself, be prepared to possibly get all banged up. But, please, realize that you are worth fighting for. You may have to constantly remind yourself and be dedicated to the commitment of: **"Whatever I have to go through for me, I am willing to do it. I am worth fighting for!"**

*You know who's gonna give you everything?
Yourself. ~ Diane von Furstenberg*

You must have *faith* in the *fight*. The battle is not intended to destroy you. The *battle* is going to *build* you. Labor through the pain. Put in the work. It is life-affirming to acknowledge that the pain is a necessary component of your healing process. You gain revelation and wisdom via your experiences. The more you live through, the more seasoned you become. Your profound experiences are purposely intended to make you better. And once you survive it, it will become only a distant afterthought. Dust off the residue from your past; reset your life. You are restored. Permit your *problems* to birth your *purpose*.

A woman, when she is in labor, has sorrow because the
hour has come; but as soon as she has given birth to the
child, she no longer remembers the anguish, for joy that a
human being has been born into the world. ~ John 16:21

Let's envision a pregnant woman grappling with insufferable contractions as she is in the throes of giving birth to her infant. Childbirth can be one of the most excruciating, painful, near-death, miraculous, humbling, selfless, loving, magnificent, spiritual acts ever experienced and/or witnessed. A laboring woman can share with you that after she travails through the delivery and the pain is over... it is just a memory.

This analysis lends itself to the explanation that although women, that have experienced childbirth, *know* how painful the process can be, many continue to have more than one child. Mothers realize that it is a *labor of love* to birth their children into this world. You must also love yourself enough to *labor through your issues. (Note: For clarification, this analogy certainly does not negate from the love and efforts of all types of parents/guardians.)*

A deep sense of gratification and pride is earned when you don't give up on yourself. You are the author of your story. Write, rewrite, edit, or better yet, **live** the narrative that candidly depicts your true self. *Your breakthrough is on the other side of your pain.*

I'm a little pencil in the hand of a
writing God. ~ Mother Teresa

The Benefits of Pain

Every adversity, every failure and every heartache
carries with it the seed of an equivalent or
a greater benefit. ~ Napoleon Hill

Facing personal agony can be a therapeutic process, but who wants to deal with pain? Well, the answer is simple. All people who truly want to authentically heal should willing tackle the challenging obstacles that they believe are the source of their suffering.

Whoever or whatever is the closest and means the most to you, has the ability to afflict you. Bravely facing the very things or people that are hurting you will allow your layers to become unpeeled. The Lord will utilize His spiritual scalpel to finely and methodically cut away every dead thing out of you and your life.

For his anger {pain} endured, but for a moment;
in his favor is life: weeping may endure for a night,
but joy cometh in the morning. ~ Psalm 30:5

This shedding procedure will assist with exposing your core. No more pretenses. No more longing to be someone or something that you are not. This rebirth affords you the opportunity to become the gregariously *real you* at all times. Abstain from fretting about life being unfair and that the stress is too much to handle. Whenever, you feel as though you are going through a bunch of crap in your life and it is basically being heaped directly on top of you, reposition yourself. Turn their crap/manure into your fertilizer. Plant seeds of love, faith, hope, focus, courage, discipline, truth, strength, and diligence. From what you once thought was simply dirt, a stunning rose will grow and bloom from the fertile soil. A beautiful exemplar that is a reward for the pain that you have endured. Strengthen your roots. Strive to blossom and flourish wherever you are planted. Always remember that anything meant for your harm, God will work it out for your benefit. You will be given beauty for your ashes.

And the day came when the risk to remain tight in a bud was more painful than the risk it took to blossom. ~ Anaïs Nin

There are true wins that you will gain from overcoming your painful circumstances. The greatest advantage is **transformation**. Your **transformation** consists of undergoing a delicate cycle of cleansing and purging. Allow yourself to undergo a complete *metamorphosis* progression. You will find your purpose on the other side of your pain.

Meta- change + **Morphosis-** form =
Allow your whole form to change.

When you give up too soon because it hurts so bad, you abort your real potential. Your mistaken belief is that there has been too much damage and no parts of you can be salvaged. Instantly, reject that notion. By God's grace and everlasting mercy, you have been revitalized and restored. Remember that *your potential, promise, and purpose is always greater than your problems.* Adjust your negative self-perception regarding pain and recognize its benefits. *Yes, pain does have benefits.* Pain has the power to literally transform you. When you perceive pain as being transformative, you begin to understand how natural it is to encounter perplexities and vicissitudes during different seasons of your life.

Pain pushes until… Vision pulls.
~ Dr. Michael Bernard Beckwith

Imagine a caterpillar. If the caterpillar had refused to surrender to its transformation, instead of being morphed into a beautiful butterfly, it would have always remained a caterpillar or stayed encased in a cocoon. If it never allowed itself to fully develop during the painful stages of being transformed, it would have never become what it was, *in essence,* created to be.

"How does one become a butterfly?" she asked pensively.
"You must want to fly so much that you are willing
to give up being a caterpillar." ~ Trina Paulus

9

When you permit the pain to be transformational, you allow your whole being to be transformed. You will no longer look like the hell that you have been through. You are mentally and emotionally strengthened. Your visioning is realized; it begins to unfold and mold you into the person you are destined to be. You become wiser, more seasoned; less reactive to things or people that do not deserve your attention or energy. You will operate on a high-frequency level.

You must go through the *struggle* in your *situation*, to gain *strength* as a *survivor*, to achieve your *success*. Some issues are a necessity. You need to go through it. You must successfully conquer those *tests* to have a *testimony*. You can triumph over any tragedy. It can be genuinely indicative to see what you are truly made of when you do not crumble under pressure.

You may encounter many defeats, but you must not be defeated. In fact, it may be necessary to encounter the defeats, so that you can know who you are, what you can rise from, how you can still come out of it. ~ Dr. Maya Angelou

---

By no means, please do not minimize the pain or be dismissive of how it has negatively affected you. Allow yourself the necessary time needed to grieve your loss or betrayal. Give yourself permission to hurt and to heal, but don't suffer longer than it is necessary. Acknowledge your wounds and then rise even more valiantly than ever before. Your testament of survival may be a courageous demonstration that could encourage or save others. Your story has the potential to provide a life-changing witness account of resiliency and endurance. I can all but guarantee you that the struggles and hurt that you survive, will absolutely help someone else.

In our own woundedness, we can become sources of life for others. ~ Henri J.M. Nouwen

---

How much can you give or circulate during your lifetime? Your emotional drudgeries were not solely meant just for you. Sometimes, it's not even about you. You were called to be a healing to others. You are equipped to motivate and make a difference in people's lives. The chronicles of your experiences can help to *elevate* humanity. Speak life into your circumstances and marvel at how God's grace will transpire throughout your life.

*God is our refuge and strength, an ever-
present help in trouble. ~ Psalm 46:1*

How can you gain wisdom if you do not withstand and persevere through misfortunes? You grow exponentially from your conflicts and afflictions. Your trials teach you about yourself. Your integrity is developed through your tribulations. Your reaction to the pain are the very tools that are required to assist with renovating and reinforcing your spiritual foundation. The challenges are building your character and competency. Each test produces fundamental keys that will be instrumental for unlocking your true calling.

*If the Son therefore shall make you free,
ye shall be free indeed. ~ John 8:36*

When you get out of your own way and do not obstruct the process, it can positively result in efficiently developing you for the *better*. Put yourself under construction; the old you need to be put through a demolition. Obliterate the self-critiquing voice that spews the despicable lie that you will never become anything more than what you currently are because of what you may have done in the past; refute the misconception that you don't deserve better because of your previous decisions and actions. Deconstruct and disregard those untruths. Some consequences may be the result of your choices, but *some things that may have happened to you are not your fault.*

Where there is ruin, there is hope for treasure. ~ Rumi

As you begin to rebuild your life, be grateful for the wisdom that you have garnered. Sifting through the debris, the shattered fragments signify that you are no longer a container that's housing past hurts. You have been loosed and freed. The broken pieces are no longer intimidating; they now represent your newfound peace. Essentially, you will go from broken *pieces to peace* when you allow God to facilitate your rebirth. Make *inner peace* your *priority*. Concede that God is using your experiences to shape and mold you into the person that you were, *in essence*, created to be.

Beware of your thoughts, they become words, Beware of your words, they become actions, Beware of your actions, they become habits, Beware of your habits, they become Character, Beware of your Character, it will become your destiny. ~ Frank Outlaw

CHARACTER:

C- ULTIVATE SELF-AWARENESS

H-OPE, HEALTH, HAPPINESS, & HUMILITY

A- NOINTING & AMBITION

R- EFLECTION & RESILIENCY

A-WAKENING & AUTHENCITY

C-HOICES, CATALYST, & CHANGE

T-RUST YOUR INTUITION/DISCERNMENT

E-LEVATED BY EXPERIENCES, EVOLVE, & EMPOWER

R-EVELATION, RELEASE, & RENEWAL

Your "Test" Will Become Your Testimony

---

*These trials have come so that your faith, being much
more precious than gold, though it be tried by fire, may
be proved genuine and may result in praise, honor, and
glory, at the appearing of Jesus Christ. ~ 1 Peter 1:7*

Once I began to realize my true worth and value, I no longer desired the things of my past. The old was passed away and I became renewed. I began to live beyond myself and to live for God. In addition to going higher, I also needed to go deeper within and rediscovered myself. I began to live my life more intentionally. Although I am an imperfect vessel, I am privileged to activate my purpose in a capacity that serves as an instrument and a representative of my Savior. I want to be a servant and a witness that loves, inspires, and leads others to Christ by sharing my testimony. Daily I pray, please use me, Lord.

---

*Behind every beautiful thing, there's
some kind of pain. ~ Bob Dylan*

God has entrusted you with the charge to take care of your soul. Each plight is a tiny step that leads to your release and awakening. No matter what you have been through, each situation was necessary. It provided the apparatuses to create who you are right now, in this moment, and the person that you are becoming.

---

*Every strike brings me closer to the
next home run. ~ Babe Ruth*

The vast majority of everything we achieve in life comes through a test. As citizens, our society's functionality is based on an influx of tests. Our educational system in its entirety is comprised of assessments. Each grade level requires a new and more rigorous exam. If you successfully pass an array of benchmarks, it indicates that you are qualified to advance unto life's next series of criterions.

To receive your driver's license, you had to take a driver's test. To obtain a role in a movie, you may have to screen test or audition. In many corporations, to be hired, applicants are required to pass a background check and/or take and pass a drug screening. When seeking employment, the interview process is about meeting the employer's requirements, the candidates must pass the organization's approval test, and only then will they be permitted to move onto the next stage. Based on your symptoms, a physician may conduct a litany of exams and blood tests to evaluate, diagnose illnesses, and/or monitor your physical well-being.

During various intervals in your lifetime, you will be subjected to taking and passing some type of examination or screening before you can proceed to the subsequent phase. These personal accomplishments are less about growth, per se, but mostly to denote that you are eligible to hold your current position; to be the person that you are. *(Note: There are levels to this.)*

Studying God's word will help to prepare you for the complexity of life's assessments. Your *Life Tests* are your testimony about receiving a passing score on your character's development. Your experience qualifies and bestows you with an established credibility. It makes you credible by stating that you have been thoroughly scrutinized and you have successfully passed life's vetting. Your personal and emotional resume' brings every background experience into account. It divulges every occurrence that God has brought you through and authenticates your history.

Do you not see how necessary a world of pains and troubles is to school an intelligence and make it a soul? ~ *John Keats*

Many of us have had our fair share of tedious journeys and endured a plethora of trials and tribulations. We are *proven* examples of what God has brought us 'through' in our lives. Our *mess* becomes our *message.* Our *tests* become our *testimony.* Our *solitude* becomes our *solace.* Our *cries* will evoke our *calling*. Our *issues* sharpen our *instincts* and enhance our *integrity*. Our *hindrances* will produce our *humility*. Our *whine* will make us a *witness* for someone else: *If God can do it for me, He can do it for you.* You were instructed to go out into all the world and be the salt of the earth. Get out of your comfort zone; you are a messenger for the Lord. Be a change agent, witness, role model, bridge-builder, trailblazer, a living example demonstrating what God is doing in your life and what He can do for others.

Our trials are for a reason. It's for us to learn and it's for us to give back to the world. ~ Cookie Johnson

---

Please recognize that everything in life happens for a reason and what is often mistaken for obstacles, were, in fact, stepping stones to lead you behind the veil. There is no need to feel inadequate or ashamed. Take the good out of every experience. *Your harshest struggles, pains, and storms, if wielded properly, can ultimately become your biggest blessings.* For each level of discord that we tackle, there is an opportunity to glean more enlightenment, more mercy, more grace, more love, more gratitude, more generosity, more compassion, more forgiveness, more acceptance, more wisdom, more hope, more possibilities, and more growth.

The problems you endure in life helps to sculpt your soul. ~ Tony Robbins

---

My personal testimony astonishes me every time I reflect upon it. I still can't believe that the Lord would save a wretch like me. When I think about His goodness and all that He's done for me, I literally get goosebumps. My life could have been destroyed. I am so grateful for the Lord's 2nd, 3rd, 4th, 5th, ... 11th, *etc.* chances. I am very cognizant of the fact that my entire circumstances could have been a tragic story. Another young lady could have endured the same exact challenges and oppositions that I have faced, but she may not have survived the calamities. It could have been me. I realize that I am very fortune and *my survival is only by the grace of God.*

The devil wanted me to remain stuck in a situation that was soiled and beneath me. Breaking every yolk and stronghold that was in my life, the Lord cast down principalities. The Lord snatched me from the snares of my adversary. God would not let the enemy have me. God canceled the enemy's plans. He never gave up on me. He has protected, guided, and kept me. I am convinced that His hand is on my life. When I call on that name, *Jesus*, my foes immediately tremble, scatter and flee from my midst. God did not allow my enemies to triumph over me. He has even blessed me in front of my haters. *I know without a doubt that it could have been different.*

And having spoiled principalities and powers, He made a show of them openly, triumphing over them. ~ Colossians 2:15

He has saved my life on numerous occasions. He has healed my body. He has shielded me from attacks that I wasn't privy to. It is only by the *blood* of Jesus that I am still here. I feel God's love, grace, mercy, and protection all over me. He has continued to bless me, *in spite of me.* Though He slay me, yet will I trust in Him forever. Regardless of what He commands, it is well with my soul. I have excelled in areas because He had already prepared the way for me. I will never doubt God's plans for my life. I am absolutely certain that there is more in store for me. I will not tarry nor waste time. I will humbly and tirelessly labor in my efforts to maximize my gifts and talents to bring forth good fruits.

God has invested too much in you for you to be comfortable in anything less than what you were created to be. ~ Bishop T.D. Jakes

Disappointments segue into appreciation and gratitude because it always works out for my good. God is so faithful. I know no good thing will the Lord withhold from me. He has kept me in my right mind. He has forgiven my transgressions. I rejoice for the generational curses that were broken in my own immediate family. I am so thankful for His presence in my life. I am indebted to Him. I owe God everything. My life is in His hands. His grace is sufficient for me. I love the Lord so much because He first loved me.

I lean on the Lord because I do not have the strength on my own. I fall to my knees in worship and give praise to Him. I cry out to the Lord and He hears me. I am a firm believer. I am forever committed to doing His will. I will put no one or nothing above the Lord. I will exalt His name all the days of my life. I can't do life without Jesus; He is the atonement and the salvation. He is the way, the truth, and the life. I am *elevated* by His forgiveness and mercy. In totality, I know that if God doesn't do it, it won't be done. He is the great, *I AM*.

For the Lord God is a sun and shield: The Lord will give grace and glory: No good thing will He withhold from them that walk uprightly. ~ Psalm 84:11

When we refuse to view the tests as potential blessings, we will continue to go through the same lessons over and over again. The lessons will be repeated until they are learned. The Holy Spirit is our tutor to help guide us through the process and the Holy Bible is the textbook that we should zealously study to show ourselves approved. *(Note: Be good stewards of God's Word.)* Although we may prefer to exempt these exams, we must rest assured that *beyond the difficulty awaits our destiny.*

The way of life winds upward for the wise. ~ Proverbs 15:24

God is exceedingly more than the world that is against you. Reprogram your thinking. Educe humility. If you are hesitant, offer your uncertainty to God and then thoroughly listen. In all of your getting, ensure that you get an understanding. Although God doesn't owe us any explanation about why we are combating different circumstances, He will give you an answer. Not only will He reply to you, but He will undoubtedly respond in a myriad of ways. When you receive God's responses, His revelations will bring conviction and should always prompt you to repent and act. (*Note: Blessed is the one whose sin the Lord will never count against them. ~ Romans 4:8*) Remember how God doubly blessed Job for his troubles. He will do the same for us when we remain faithful and put our trust in Him.

By three methods we may learn wisdom: First, by reflection, which is noblest, second, by imitation, which is the easiest; and third, by experience, which is the bitterest. ~ Confucius

Transpose your stumbling blocks, that were once perceived to be obstacles, into stepping stones toward future prospects. Those same stones are going to *elevate* your platform. Remember that the stone that the builders rejected, ultimately became the chief corner stone. We can wreak havoc when we insist upon being in complete control. Change the lens in which you interpret your conditions. Shift your mindset. Rid yourself of narrow-minded thinking. Allow your mind's eye to view any predicaments or rejections as God's grace, protection, and redirection in your life. Trust in the Lord and His perfect timing.

God is able to do exceeding abundantly above all that we ask or think. ~ Ephesians 3:20

Pain, Purpose, and Power

Challenges are what make life interesting, and overcoming them is what makes life meaningful. ~ Joshua J. Marine

---

To be effective, the process of working through your pain must be a consistent continuation. You need to feel the pain, in order, to heal, but please do not dwell in it. Do not give up too soon and possibly miss the reward. To rectify and conquer your *vices*, you must go behind the *veil*. Your *problems* will produce a *plan* that will become your *platform*. Your *fight* builds your *fortitude*. Your *mourning* will become your *mission/ movement*. Your *treasure* is behind your *trash*. Your *burdens* will become your *blessings*. Your *frustrations* will establish your *foundation*. Your *sorrow* will make you *stronger*. Your *setbacks* will enhance your *skills*. Your *struggles* and *strife* are used to *shape* you. Your *failures* will enhance your *focus*. Your *losses* are your *lessons*. Your *wounds* will become your *wisdom*. Your *adversity* will work to your *advantage*.

Your *challenges* and *chaos* will stimulate your *creativity*. Your *troubles* will develop your *tenacity*. Your *issues* will cultivate your *integrity*. Your *famine* will transition into your *favor*. Your *anger* will fuel your *accomplishments*. Your *stress* will create your *success*. Your *misery* will become your *ministry*. Your *enemies* will *energize* and *empower* you. Your *persecution* is the *preparation* that will elevate you into your new *position*. Your *oppositions* are your *opportunities*. Your *vicissitudes* will provide clarity for your *vision*. Your *disasters* shall guide you in the direction towards your *destiny*. Your *agony* will put you in *alignment* with your *awakening*. Your *seeking* of the Lord will lead to your *self-awareness* and *self-renewal*. On the other side of your *pain* lies your *purpose* and *power*.

The heavens declare the glory of God; the skies proclaim the work of His hands. ~ Psalm 19:1

For instance, have you ever paid attention to a severe thunderstorm? Take a moment to picture everything that a bad storm may entail. The dark ominous clouds, howling winds, roaring thunderbolts, and electrifying lightning produces a terrifying backdrop. The rain is so heavy that it appears to be falling in sheets. Extreme flooding can convert streets into raging rivers. The vehemence combination of the gusts of wind and precipitation are so aggressively strong; it has the strength to uproot, blow over, wash away, or snap anything in its path. The inclement weather can cause utter devastation. And if you are ever stuck amidst an extreme storm, it can be truly frightening, or in some unfortunate cases, even fatal.

> *The greater the difficulty, the more glory in surmounting it. Skillful pilots gain their reputation from storms and tempests. ~ Epictetus*

Well, the thunderstorm may be symbolic of the commotion that is currently unfurling in your life and the pain represents the remnants of disarray that has constantly agonized you over time. The darken skylines of your life falsely insinuate that you will never bask in sunshine, love, happiness, or wholeness again. You cannot foresee anything good coming from your suffering.

> *Life isn't about waiting for the storm to pass, it's about learning to dance in the rain. ~ Vivian Greene*

You may feel that the agony is too much to bear and it will ultimately be the basis of your entire undoing. The initial turmoil seems too devastating. You believe that there is absolutely no chance that you can survive these depressing, catastrophic conditions. It has all become too tormenting. You brace for the convulsive impact that will accompany the impending doom.

And a great windstorm arose... Then He arose and
rebuked the wind, and said to the sea, "Peace, be
still!" And the wind ceased and there was a great calm...
He said to them, "Why are you so fearful? How is
it that you have no faith?" And they feared exceedingly,
and said to one another, "Who can this be, that even
the wind and the sea obey Him!" ~ Mark 4:37-41

Upon reflection, have you ever witnessed the end-result of a harrowing thunderstorm? The aftermath is in stark contrast of the before and during effects of the turbulent weather. The horizon is a stunning canvas that artistically exhibits the fluffy white and luscious clouds. Vivid sunshine cascades among the heavenly, blue skies beaming luminous sunrays spanning broadly across every surface of your surroundings. The sun gently plants warm, tender kisses on your forehead. Your skin becomes golden and tanned because it has been kissed by the sun. Trees sway in the wind, while their leaves playfully wave at you. A cool, light breeze casually tickles the tip of your nose. Birds can be heard cheerily chirping a melodious tune. Then to perfectly illuminate this breathtaking, gorgeous scenery, and to add the most beautiful blessing of all, a stunning, colorful, vibrant, mystical, riveting rainbow may even appear. *Wow! Look, at God's grace.*

I have set my rainbow in the clouds, and it will be the sign
of the covenant between Me and the earth. ~ Genesis 9:13

After you have gone through your *'storms'* and faced your pain, you will be purified, intensified, and edified. The striking colors of your rainbow will become evident and reflected through your character. Isn't that such a profound comparison? Some of our best lessons are the result of our seemingly worst trials and tribulations. *(Note: Storms make trees take deeper roots. ~ Dolly Parton)* Some of our worst sufferings can produce our greatest blessings. God can bring order to our pandemonium; He will never give us more than we can handle.

(Note: Always remember that your God is bigger than any storm that you may face.)

We should glory in the trials and tribulations,
knowing that the tribulation produces perseverance.
And perseverance, character; and character, hope.
New hope does not disappoint, because the love of
God has been poured out in our hearts by the Holy
Spirit who was given to us. ~ Romans 5:3-5

You *need* to be whole. You *deserve* to be whole. Your character should be fulfilled and not lacking in any area. When you are complacent about confronting your pain, the suffering phase will continue to hold you in captivity. You must *face the pain* and *conquer it*. It is a part of your mission. There is a divine assignment for your life. Your problems and pain have a designed purpose. God wants to give you a breakthrough. He must *break* you so that you will be *through* with whatever is keeping you bound. You had to be *broken,* in order, to be a *blessing.* And even in all of your *brokenness,* you are still *beautiful.*

Though He brings grief, He will show
compassion. ~ Lamentations 3:31-32

The grace of God will open your eyes. Each experience was essential. Nothing that you have endured will be in vain; nothing will be wasted. Surviving your darkest times, makes you shine the brightest. Each new morning will bring you a new joy. All your quandaries were the ingredients that contributed to making you the person that you are today. You are the conduit that the Creator is going to skillfully and creatively use to help edify and empower others.

In times of great stress or adversity, it's always
best to keep busy, to plow your anger and your
energy into something positive. ~ Lee Iacocca

Envisage the image that you want to project. Show up and present yourself in the manner of how you wish to be perceived. Establish expectations and standards that are non-negotiable. *"Inspect what you expect"* of yourself; conduct mini self-assessments to monitor the progress of your new pain-survival lifestyle. You must continue to strive to grow, evolve, and inspire others. You will subsist the pain and become a better and whole person because of it. Now, here is a little catch: **Do not return to or attempt to restore whatever God has released you from.** *If He brought you out... stay out.* Your *purpose* and *power* lie just on the other side of the *pain.* Keep moving forward, onward, and upward.

For I reckon that the sufferings of this present
time are not worthy to be compared with the glory
which shall be revealed in us. ~ Romans 8:18

It's Over: Forgive Yourself for Past Mistakes

If pain must come, may it come quickly. Because
I have a life to live, and I need to live it in
the best way possible. ~ Paulo Coelho

Do you ever wish that you could go back and change a certain situation? Are you having a hard time forgiving yourself for a decision that you made in your past? Well, you are not alone. Everyone, at some point, has made regrettable blunders that we wish could miraculously be eradicated from our history. And if you have not had a calamitous experience yet, just keep living... one is likely to occur.

The truth is that any struggles that you faced, those good or bad experiences, are the product, typically, of the choices that you have made. Generally, your circumstances are predicated upon your decisions. Your choices precede every action or reaction that you have. If you make deliberate choices, you may become less reactive toward various provocations. Pray continually for the Lord to guide your choices and to help you stand firm in the decisions that you make.

If something happens to you, with a clear mind, you can choose how to rationally respond. You are less likely to blame others for what may culminate into an unpleasant situation. (*Note: There are instances where certain painful situations were not your fault. You should not harbor guilt nor allow anger to fester due to the pain inflicted upon you because of the actions of others.*)

Let every man be swift to hear, slow to speak,
slow to wrath; for the wrath of man does not
produce righteous of God. ~ James 1:19-20

Do not permit your past mistakes to have access to the power that can hold you hostage. Do not grant your past the liberty to make you live as a prisoner. Never become gratified with remaining idle. The shackles of your past will no longer have control. The restraints don't have the authority to keep you bound. You are more than what you have been through. In fact, if you allow the process to run its course, you will be made whole and better *because of* what you've been through. It may be cliché to say that *"everything happens for a reason"*, but it is true. You just need to be strategic about identifying the specific reason.

Who of you by worrying can add a single
hour to his life? ~ Matthew 6:27

Experience is an unbiased teacher. *She* is unconcerned with demographics, vitals, status, race, income, zip codes, affiliations, etc. *She* is only focused on teaching *her* lesson. You cannot take what has happened to you personally. It is a tutorial and to move forward to the next level or graduate, you need to master the curricula. If you do not want to remain trapped in the remedial class of life, it is mandatory that you successfully excel the course.

In school, you're taught a lesson and then given a test. In life,
you're given a test that teaches you a lesson. ~ Unknown

Your faith doesn't make you immune to conflicts; your faith helps to assure you that you can overcome any, and all, challenges. You must allow your wounds to properly heal and accept that your scars are a part of your strength. They are subtle reminders of your endurance and victory. Please do not remain captive to your past. You cannot change what has happened 10 years, 10 days, or even 10 minutes ago. *It happened; it is over.* You must acknowledge the circumstances, glean from the curriculum, and leave the *teacher* behind.

*There is no greater battle in life than the battle
between the parts of you that want to be healed and
the parts of you that are comfortable and content
with remaining broken. ~ Iyanla Vanzant*

Your past does not define you. You are more than a conqueror; you are a warrior and a champion. In everything that you combat, no matter the event, you can learn something from it. Shed the weight by ridding yourself of that old baggage. At some point, you will get so tired of carrying those burdens around. You can't even begin to realize how heavy it's been this entire time until you finally release it. No matter what you have ever done... God *can* and *will* use you, anyway. *You* are God's amazing creation. *You* are His awe-inspiring workmanship. You were not formed to just exist. You are not here by accident. Everything that you have been through is for a particular purpose. The Lord has plans for you.

*"For I know the plans I have for you", declares the
Lord, "plans to prosper you and not to harm you, plans
to give you hope and a future." ~ Jeremiah 29:11*

The evolution from your experiences will set the trajectory that will propel you into your future. You are on the launching pad toward your destiny. To fully commit to authenticity, it is imperative to become the person that you were meant to be. Love who you are. *Love you for you.* Do not veer away from what makes you original, special and unique. Because at the end of the day, *you* have to live with yourself and your decisions.

When you are sad or make mistakes, it is intuitive that you reassess, because it is a warning sign or a wake-up call that you may need to readjust. *(Note: What is your life trying to tell you?... Are you listening?)* It indicates that you are not where you need to be at that particular point of your journey. You may have to change your navigation. It may be necessary to pivot, take an alternative course, detour or reroute your pathway. Do not allow pain to pave a path towards your purpose. When you come to that faithful fork in the road, be very mindful of selecting the best direction. Choose and stay in the lane that leads to your promise.

We come this way only but once. We can either tiptoe through life and hope that we get to death without being too badly bruised or we can live a full, complete life achieving our goals and realizing our wildest dreams. ~ Bob Proctor

Forgiveness must become a part of your arsenal of resources to help release you from your past faults. Forgiveness is therapeutic; it is a state of mind; a rare form of simply *being*. No matter what you have done, you can be forgiven. The most challenging aspect is that *you must forgive yourself*. Do not continue to hyperbolize past situations, instead set upon a mission of absolving any prevalent matters that could eventually set you free.

I have lived a long life and had many troubles, most of which never happened. ~ Mark Twain

It is also vital that we forgive others. Holding onto past hurts and grudges can be toxic and only exacerbates the pain. When we truly forgive, this freedom empowers us to be receptive of grace, acceptance, restoration, authentic happiness, and it also provides an opportunity to love more deeply. We will no longer replay scenarios in our mind of how we wish things would be, but begin to justly accept them for how they truly are. Forgiveness reminds us of God's mighty power and presence that reigns supreme in our own lives.

As long as you don't forgive, who and whatever it is will occupy rent-free space in your mind. ~ Isabelle Holland

At times, it may seem that you have hit rock bottom and may never recover. Just remember the axiom, *"it's okay to hit rock bottom, as long as Jesus is the rock."* Create a clean slate, a new foundation, and begin afresh. You could have withstood some of the cruelest sufferings that may be too painful to even mention, but you are a survivor and an overcomer. You have endured because you have a divine purpose and promise to fulfill. You were being stretched, but you did not break. You are much stronger than you believe.

Rock bottom became the solid foundation on which I rebuilt my life. ~ JK Rowling

---

The *new* you and the *old* you cannot co-exist at the same time. You must emancipate one or the other. There is no half-way in or out. You cannot straddle the fence and live a double life, but instead, should become very clear about the type of existence that you are committed to creating for yourself. When you embrace who you **were** and recognize who you **are** evolving into, you must acknowledge that you should not try to completely separate the two individuals.

Your past persona and your current being are both vital for your future survival. You do not have to forget where you come from, and you shouldn't, because it provides valuable data. But, likewise, you should not allow the previous residue to taint your immeasurable promises. Be prepared to appraise where you are and strategize where you want to go. Then you must conceive and execute a plan of action to get there. You should embody a strong sense of faith, love, self-awareness, and chutzpah. Take immediate ownership for creating the life that you desire.

One thing I do: Forgetting those things which are behind, and reaching forth unto those things which are before. I press toward the mark for the prize of the high calling God in Christ Jesus. ~ Philippians 3:13 -14

Can you alter the past? No. But, you can make peace with it and move forward. Your yesterday no longer has the influence to make you feel guilty or humiliated. You should no longer be embarrassed about prior errs because you live, you learn, and must not repeat the pattern. *(Note: In some cases, you may need to unlearn some things.)* Mistakes make you wiser and help you to become more of who you are meant to be. Refute the dogma that your situation will never get better. The opposite of evolving is inertia. Direct your solicitude toward making your tomorrow a new beginning. Focus only on what is in front of you.

An advantage of outlasting the pain is that naiveté is no longer an option. You become seasoned and emboldened to make informed decisions. You have been changed and transformed. You can fully embrace and love the 'real you'. To cultivate a level of transparency, you must set the authentic intentions that will serve as the key preparations for your future possibilities.

The secret of change is to focus all your energy not on fighting the old, but on building the new. ~ Socrates

Chapter I: Pain and Past Mistakes
Self-Coaching Session

1. Are you currently enduring a painful situation? What strategies are you employing to help you overcome these challenges?

2. Have you overcome formidable circumstances and have become better because of it? How were you able to make a successful comeback?

3. Have you ever shared your story/testimony, in an effort, to help someone else? Why or why not?

4. What advice could you give to someone that is encountering the same struggles that you have faced?

5. What specific intentions could you set today that will allow your test to become a testimony to uplift, inspire and empower someone else?

Chapter I: Pain and Past Mistakes
Self-Reflection Notes

CHAPTER II

$\mathcal{Elevated}$ BY
BEING BALANCED

*A wise woman recognizes when her life is out of balance
and summons the courage to act to correct it, she knows the
meaning of true generosity, happiness is the reward for a life
lived in harmony, with a courage and grace. ~ Suze Orman*

Forgetting to Put Yourself on the "To-Do" List

*Self-care is never a selfish act. It is simply good
stewardship of the only gift I have, the gift I was put
on earth to offer to others. ~ Parker Palmer*

I was so tired of feeling lost. I had always put other people's interests before my own. I was a poster child for the *"forgetting to put yourself on the list"* pattern. I was in a relationship where I could prepare my significant other's favorite dish to perfection. What was my preferred meal? Nothing in particular... What was his favorite color? Blue. What was my favorite color? I wasn't certain, maybe I did not have one... I was an expert concerning his needs but neglected my own. Everything centered around my family and career. Practically, before any formal or informal decision was finalized, I would obtain their approval. Whenever my agenda conflicted with their schedules, without any hesitation, I would reschedule or cancel my plans. There was no need for dissension, my first obligation was to my family, even if at times, my allegiance to them posed an inconvenience for me. I felt as if I had lost my identity. *I failed to make myself a priority.*

*It's not selfish to love yourself, take care of yourself, and
make your happiness a priority.
It's necessary. ~ Mandy Hale*

I combatted many complications and muddled through numerous challenges. I had to make various heartrending decisions. I was doing what I perceived that I liked, but *I did not like what I was doing.* I finally came to a breaking point. My overwhelming need to seek self-fulfillment was a wake-up call. I realized for me to personally and professionally ascend and advance, it was critical that I make some immediate, difficult modifications. I needed to put first things *first* in my life. I had to *get myself together.*

Either you run the day, or the day runs you. ~ *Jim Rohn*

My childhood involved being rooted in the church. A redemptive turning point for me was being able to recall what I learned from my strong, spiritual background. I regurgitated those principles and practices that I garnered in my youth. I promptly recalibrated and incorporated those strategies into my life. It was literally, without a doubt, my saving grace.

It is also a blessing to know that someone is potentially praying and interceding for us. Sometimes when we get in "trouble", we want to *run away* from God until 'we make everything perfect'; but, that is precisely the time to *run to* God. He cares so deeply for us; He is comforting and compassionate. He wants to help. It was this seed that was planted within that motivated me to *"look to the hills from whence cometh my help. {And know that} My help cometh from the Lord."* ~ *Psalms 121:1-2.*

Innately, you should replenish yourself, nourish your intellect, and develop your own pastimes independent of your family and career. You possess the freedom to establish your own distinctive identity, impartial to others' personalities or biases. Most rewardingly, being your own person, makes you more interesting. By lending your voice, you can participate in engaging, thought-provoking discussions and contribute your perspective. You are the primary stakeholder in your life and your input on how it is lived is invaluable.

I am sick and tired of being sick and
tired. ~ *Fannie Lou Hamer*

With determination, I decided to make vast improvements in my life. I ended some relationships, made important career changes, and became diligent about keeping regular appointments with myself. If we have the audacity to regularly maintenance our vehicle, to ensure that it is running efficiently and smoothly, we must put forth an even more, conscious effort in maintaining ourselves. We are God's vessel. This is the only body and mind that we will ever have. Our bodies carry us around daily; it is our temple. We must be good to it.

In addition, begin to adopt a spiritual practice. You should incessantly think healthy thoughts, pray and meditate. It is absolutely imperative that you take care of yourself. You may be imitated, but you can never be duplicated. *There will only ever be just one of you. Only one. You are an original.* So, not completely taking care of yourself, is not an option.

The one thing that you have that nobody else has is you. Your voice, your mind, your story, your vision. So write, draw, build, play, dance, and live as only you can. ~ Neil Gaiman

---

Are You Giving More than You Are Receiving?

> *The most painful thing is losing yourself in the*
> *process of loving someone too much, and forgetting*
> *that you are special too. ~ Ernest Hemingway*

How many hats do you wear? Do you assume so many roles that, at times, you lose count? So many of us are guilty of overwhelming ourselves with numerous responsibilities and obligations. We are practically bogged down with our own issues, and then we begin to take on other people's affairs. We let other individuals' *'emergencies'* become *our problem.*

Are you familiar with the gripe, *"If it isn't one thing, it's another?"* Well, it doesn't have to be that way, unless you condone these dilemmas. Of course, this refers to the situations that you have control over. And whatever you don't have control over, you should release it to the Lord. At some point in our lives, many of us have been guilty of giving more than we have received. At times, we aren't even aware of this behavior. Typically, sometimes, givers must hit a brick wall before they realize that they have ignored the previous warning signs.

> *When people show you who they are, believe*
> *them... the first time. ~ Dr. Maya Angelou*

Let's utilize a car analogy as a demonstration. *You* represent the car. You begin your week on a full tank of gas. You go about your normal routine of commuting to and from work, as well as running several errands. At some point, you found yourself driving your family and friends around like you are a part-time chauffeur or taxi driver for *free.* Throughout the week, with the surge of extraneous transporting duties, you never stopped to refuel, nor did anyone offer to provide you with gas money or fare. By the end of the week, you are oblivious that you are running off of fumes until the car *(you)* breaks down and completely runs out of gas leaving you stranded. Anyone privy to this scenario would not be surprised at your inevitable immobility. No one except maybe, you. You were only doing what you have always done, being accessible and accountable for everyone else's needs.

It is essential that you proclaim that all things in your life operate on an equal transaction basis. There must be a balance, a fair exchange. This does not lend itself to the roles that are a priority in your life, such as a mother, wife, partner, proprietor, etc. But the key word is *priority*. These positions should automatically feed your soul in return. Let's delve deeper to evaluate their contributions.

It's all about quality of life and finding a happy balance between work and friends and family. ~ Philip Green

It is vital that you tap into your authentic self and determine your limitations. You must model your expectations. Your words and actions have merit. I am a strong advocate of the sentiment that, *you teach people how to treat you*. People do not know your boundaries. They will continue to *take* as long as you continue to *give*. By the same token, will you continue to *give* as long as they continue to *take*? What are your motives? Do you have a desire to feel needed? Does having control over certain situations appeal to you? It can beget a vicious, addictive cycle.

It is important to assess whether you garner a sense of fulfillment from being a hero or martyr to others. At times, you may feel that it is your duty to go above and beyond for your loved ones (and sometimes, even for those that are not your loved ones) because you want them to be happy. You have convinced yourself that if they're happy, you're happy or that your feelings do not matter. It is even possible, that you may just want to placate others to keep the peace. Either assumption would suggest that you tread lightly. These are deprecating territories that should be avoided.

I've learned that people will forget what you said,
people will forget what you did, but people will never
forget how you made them feel. ~ Dr. Maya Angelou

As a giver, nurturer or supporter, you must set limits because a taker will not. Why should they? You must establish those parameters. If you do not, then you may become a resentful enabler. You have always been placid and carefully guarded. But when you harbor so many unreleased issues and you are not receiving the proper intake that is equivalent to your outtake, implosive bombs are formed. What you have begrudgingly tolerated inwardly, will manifest itself outwardly. The frustrations fester until simmering and percolating are no longer an option, and then you just explode. Because you have previously hidden your anger so well, individuals may become confused, stunned or even offended at your sudden, volatile outburst.

Establish high standards and do not lower them for anyone; do not reduce your self-worth. People will try to degrade what they didn't contribute to. It is easy for others to try to cheapen or shortchange a person or a position when they don't know or understand the real cost. *Don't discount your dignity.* If others insist that you are expecting far too much, reiterate, *as often as you deem necessary,* that true value, self-respect, integrity, and inner peace *never* goes on sale or clearance.

You must be cautious of whom and what you are giving yourself to. Therefore, it is important to know *who* you are, *Whose* you are, and to discover your *why* in life. Do not disregard your own feelings. You are not a superhero; you are human. You also have your own needs. Follow your own moral compass. What are your priorities, capabilities, and limitations? You need to ensure that you are taking your own ambitions into consideration before you continuously oblige others. You must know and love yourself before you can share these qualities with someone else.

Go to the Lord in prayer. With sincerity, ask Him to expose *you* to *you*; to help you discover your God-assigned identity. What do you like about yourself? What do you truly need? What efforts do you need to exert? How can you be more consistent? It is crucial that you take care of yourself. There is the popular quote, "there is no **"I"** in *team*," but in the same vein, there **is** an **"U"** in *you/yourself*. It is great to be a team player and contribute, but the deeds must be reciprocated. If you do not take care of *yourself*, you will not be very effective for any team. When you give more than you receive, it is only a matter of time before the bottom line will result in you becoming tapped out, exhausted, and possibly even bitter.

Let's envision another hypothetical situation. You are a financial institution. As a bank, you are constantly allowing withdrawals to be taken out of your (*life*) account. There are no deposits being contributed to the bank (*you*). When payments are not made at the same frequent pace as the amount of the withdrawals, an *overdraft* will occur in your life because of the insufficient funds (*contributions*). You will no longer possess assets, but instead, acquire liabilities. You will become (*emotionally*) bankrupt. You must *pre-qualify* the individuals that will have access to you. Ensure that you are being fairly recompensed for your *investments* into others. *Audit* your relationships and review the *receipts*. Are you receiving a Return on Investments *(ROI)*?

People were created to be loved. Things were created to be used. The reason why the world is in chaos, is because things are being loved, and people are being used. ~ John Green

---

Wherever you deem to be worthy enough to contribute your time, energy, love, finances to, those areas should provide you with an impartial compensation for your efforts. This goes beyond monetary exchanges. Does it give you happiness, joy, love, peace, hope, stability, or provides you with a sense of purpose, etc.? There should be a level of replenishment involved.

If you are giving more than you are receiving, you must confront any inconsistencies and make immediate changes. Being uncomfortable with making hard decisions, may ultimately disrupt your destiny. Rethink your relationships. If these people truly respected you, then their efforts would be equivalent to yours. They should be dispensing nearly, if the not more than, the same amount of emotions and energies.

Surround yourself with people that are invested in you and those that you can wholeheartedly invest in.

This above all: To thine own self be true. ~ Hamlet

Perhaps, this is why self-reflection is so vital. A candid appraisal will disclose any deficiencies. If there are situations or people in your life that are saboteurs, energy stealers, manipulators, temporary, or out-of-season individuals, you are going to have to make the firm choice to sever ties and move forward. You can no longer be weighed down. You must establish restrictions. Regulate how much you give to others and in addition, practice the subtle art of receiving. Summon the courage to reassign the roles in your life. Make it mandatory that there must be a fair exchange/reciprocity. There will be no exceptions.

You Are a Priority

---

*It took me quite a long time to develop a voice, and now that
I have it, I am not going to be silent. ~ Madeleine Albright*

Sometimes you do not give yourself enough credit for the accomplishments/goals that you have achieved. Apparently, at times, you can become so embroiled in your past experiences or present mundane day-to-day busy life that you overlook how far you have come. You allow yourself to go out of your way, above and beyond expectations for others, but will not extend the same courtesy to yourself. Often, you really do not view yourself as a priority. Becoming so fixated with checking off your tasks of completion, you forget to put **YOU** on your *To-Do* list.

---

*There's nothing wrong with being driven. And there's
nothing wrong with putting yourself first to reach your
goals. The other stuff still happens. ~ Shonda Rhimes*

It would be selfish, to put your needs before others, right? *No.* If *you* do not take care of *you, you* will not be capable of taking care of others. You must recondition your mindset. You must realize that you are important, too. In the case of an emergency, what is one of the most valuable safety tips that a flight attendant advises if you are traveling with small children? You are directed to put the oxygen mask on *your face first*, and then you may put it on your child. It would not be beneficial if you were to pass out trying to put the mask on the child first. If you faint, both of you will be rendered helpless. It is critical that you take care of yourself. You must make yourself a priority in your own life. *You* are your primary objective.

One of the most courageous things you can do is identify
yourself, know who you are, what you believe in and
where you want to go. ~ Sheila Murray Bethel

One of the biggest and most worthwhile challenges that you may struggle with is to heal the wounds of your past. Although you may have made some unfavorable mistakes, it would be an utter fabrication to believe that your discretions were so atrocious that you are no longer significant; that somehow you are now unworthy. Life is a resourceful teacher. Take 100% responsibility and make peace with your erroneousness. Do not blame others. You must be accountable for your actions. We are each liable for our own lives. We must learn from our faults, grow from the experiences, and become a better person because of each lesson.

You must take personal responsibility. You cannot
change the circumstances, the seasons, or the wind,
but you can change yourself. ~ Jim Rohn

Purposely, do not lose interest in your life. It is imperative that you do not become stagnant and complacent. You should not robotically follow a simple, bland routine. If you opt-out of being engaged in the sophisticated intricateness that is blissfully interwoven within the fabrics of your inner being, your total existence will become unfulfilling, dull, and desensitized. Reject conformity by resolving to be recusant to traditional behavior. Opt to live a full life by taking risks and making new discoveries about yourself. Disregard any backlash from your critics. Because at this exact moment, for once, your needs are of the utmost importance. You have just as much right to be as ecstatically happy as anyone else. Do not wait for happiness to find you; go and get it. You deserve to be happy *right now*.

*Your journey begins with a choice to get up, step out,
and live fully. Whether you flounder or flourish is
always in your hands. More important than 20/20
eyesight is your internal vision, your spirit whispering
through your life its guidance and grace. YOU are the
single biggest influence in your life. ~ Oprah Winfrey*

Establish the theme for your life. As the author of your story, you have the power to rehash and emphasize certain topics for the most effect or you can make edits to your storyline before transcribing any additional descriptive sentences or scenes. You could literally write a new chapter at any point that you choose to. Be mindful of not writing from the perspective of your pain. Do not put a period where there should only be a comma or a semicolon. Your story does not have to be anticlimactic. It should be exciting, adventurous, a little mysterious, with the inclusion of alluring arcs, and serendipitous plot twists. Habitually, write daily, and when you need to refocus or revise, you can either turn the page or momentarily pause by inserting *"To Be Continued..."* Most importantly, only your creative, collaborative writing partner and editor, *God*, can authorize any alternate, surprise endings.

*Every sunrise is like a new page, a chance to receive
each day in all its glory. ~ Oprah Winfrey*

You deserve a life where each day is a fresh start to seek infinite promises. You are thriving and not simply, just surviving. Learn to appreciate yourself, honor your spirit, raise your vibrations, and amp up your high-frequency levels. When you extend positive energy, it becomes reciprocal. You will acquire more courage by simply *showing up*. Show up for your life. Enjoy each day.

Sit. Feast on Your Life. ~ Derek Walcott

What Makes You Happy?

*If you look at what you have in life, you'll always
have more. If you look at what you don't have in
life, you'll never have enough. ~ Oprah Winfrey*

What do you want out of life? What makes you feel alive? What makes you leap out of bed in the mornings? Are you living a life that you love? A life that is fulfilling and brings you joy. Are you the person that you yearn to be? Are you constantly maturing and emerging into a newer and better version of yourself? Are you fostering an environment that is supportive of your lifestyle and choices? Are you surrounding yourself with positivity? Are you partaking in calisthenics activities and a nutritious diet to ensure that you are maintaining your health? Daily, are you engaging in specific acts that give you immense happiness? Are you following your passion and fulfilling your purpose? Aristotle posed the prolific question, *"How shall we live in order to be happy?"* Intentionally, each day, begin to do more of what makes you happy.

*It is not uncommon for people to spend their whole
life waiting to start living. ~ Eckhart Tolle*

Life doesn't just start to happen when you decide it is the "right time". Please do not delay what you would really like to do with your life until what you perceive to be the "right opportunity". The right time to start is *now*. Stop procrastinating; time is continuously passing. You are in denial if you believe that tomorrow is promised to any of us. This exact moment is something that you will never be able to get back again. There will never truly be a convenient time to start an endeavor. Every instant, every thought, every decision, and every initiative helps to shape your destiny. Research has proven that there is a direct link between identifying the happiest people as those that are living full and meaningful lives. Their intentional decisions have guided them into creating an authentic existence.

At times, regardless of how difficult it may seem, you must be candid with yourself. Are you operating as a simulation of someone else? Are you being your most authentic self? Does your inner being match your outer being? What are you truly made of? If you were to take the mask off would you recognize your true self? You must connect with the truth. There is power in the truth. Do not be too hard on yourself if you discover some cracks in your foundation. It is all about the development. *(Note: Forget your perfect offering. There's a crack, a crack in everything. That's how the light gets in. ~ Leonard Cohen)* Do not judge yourself or others. Get rid of any domineering, negative thoughts that may try to hinder your self-improvement.

No {more}stinking thinking. ~ Zig Ziglar

There is not a magical starting point to begin to live a fulfilled life. You do not have to accomplish anything specific *(e.g., get a new house, buy a car, get married, get divorced, obtain a degree, become rich, lose weight, gain weight, get a new hairstyle, become perfect, etc.)* to receive joy, happiness, or to become complete. Protect your heart and your peace. Be selective about who or what you allow to have a front row seat in your life. Everyone does not deserve an invitation; any negative associations may have a lasting effect. You do not need any interruptions, so separation may be the best tactic. Be protective of your space. You deserve happiness. Become defiant if necessary, by absolutely refusing to settle for anything less.

Joy is your birthright. I encourage you to claim it. ~ Vanessa K. De Luca

---

Joy is derived from doing what you were created to do. Finding your purpose and succeeding in the space of intentionality. *(Note: You can have more than one purpose.)* Success constitutes being able to enjoy what you're doing, live what you love, and being giddy, *yes, delightfully giddy,* about life. Luxuriating in the land of self-awareness, you feel engulfed by inner peace. Strongly discerning that somehow you are in the right place, at the right time. The revelation of the audacious avowals … *"I was made for this"* and *"I belong here"* are confirmations that you have found your sweet spot. Your exhilaration is firing up on all cylinders. Only idyllic thoughts and feelings are etched into your heart and mind. You have made the conscientious decision to be intentional about the quality of life that you desire and deserve.

Generally, accomplishing this level of euphoria does not happen overnight. Honestly, you may not even recognize the precise instant that it materializes. You literally have an epiphany and suddenly realize that you are ridiculously content, at peace, and actually *living* what you love. Take gradual steps and organically gain momentum. Allow yourself to formulate mini-happiness successes so that you are more prone to continue your quest. Develop the stamina to endure the rollercoaster ride. There will be peaks and valleys. Ensure that you are disciplined and focused. Your evolution will continuously unfold and be revealed as you accomplish your goals while simultaneously exploring along the newly created paths to discover your destiny.

Learn how to be happy with what you have while
you pursue all that you want. ~ Jim Rohn

If you do not truly value yourself, who else will? Simply focus on the type of life that you dream of; you have the authority to go about the business of creating it. You are the architect of your own life; design it in such a way that it brings you the utmost pleasure and excitement each day. You deserve a new beginning. Start your journey to happiness now. Learn how to show up for yourself. It may not be easy, but it will definitely be worth it. *YOU Are Worth It.*

Happiness is when what you think, what you say, and
what you do are in harmony. ~ Mahatma Gandhi

10 Thought-Provoking Guiding Questions to
Help Discover What Makes You Happy

1. *What are the "little things" that make you happy?*

2. *What makes you happy in your personal relationships?*

3. *What makes you happy in your professional relationships/career?*

4. *What is something about yourself that initially made you cringed, but now you fully accept?*

5. *What are some areas that you perceive are currently lacking in your life?*

6. *What are some challenges that are causing an obstruction to your happiness?*

7. *What is something that you would "change/fix" if you could "do it all over again"?*

8. *Who or what is no longer a good fit and should be eliminated from your life?*

9. *What is your ideal personal and/or professional relationship?*

10. *What would you describe as a seemingly perfect day in your life?*

Ponder your responses to these questions. Contemplate what these answers mean to you. What were you able to glean that aroused the most edifying *"aha"* moment? After analyzing your findings, create a *Happiness* journal or utilize the *Self-Reflection Notes* section to record your results. Next, specify which productive action steps that you could implement in your life today to achieve your desired outcomes.

Establishing Boundaries

---

*Never make someone a priority when all you are
to them is an option. ~ Dr. Maya Angelou*

As previously mentioned, I am a firm proponent of the belief that, *"you teach people how to treat you."* Clear and concise boundaries must be established to certify that you do not end up emotionally bankrupted. Referencing our prior bank account analogy, recall the detriment that can occur because of misappropriating assets *(the lack of: love, efforts, respect, appreciation...)*. The deficit investments contribute to the imbalance of withdrawals and deposits, which causes your account *(you)* to become overdrawn. If you are constantly making *withdrawals,* but are not making substantial *deposits*, you are going to end up with *insufficient funds.* When you unselfishly *give, give,* and *give,* but do not inherit any comparable sums *(efforts)* in exchange, then inevitably, your account will incur a negative balance *(anger/bitterness/resentment).* If you do not replenish, you are going to end up depleted. There must be an equitable transaction.

---

*If you spend your life sparing people's feelings and
feeding their vanity, you get so you can't distinguish what
should be respected in them. ~ F. Scott Fitzgerald*

You cannot be accessible to everyone else and not be available for yourself. Someone will always need something. They will always need a favor. They will attempt to make their emergencies and lack of planning become your problem. Instead of learning from their repeated mistakes and becoming wiser, they look to you to bail them out of their irresponsible messes.

Periodically, conduct an appraisal of your obligations and relationships to decipher which persons are being inconsiderate of your personal endeavors and responsibilities. *You need to audit your inner circle.* Keep abreast of these certain coercers that will latch on and zap all of your energy, time, and financial means without an iota of respect for what you may have going on in your own life. It is always about what they need from you. When you sacrifice your itinerary to accommodate their every whim, you are literally sabotaging yourself. Utilize your discernment, to weed these *temporary* people out of your life. They have become *out-of-season* individuals.

When we fail to set boundaries and hold people accountable,
we feel used and mistreated. This is why we sometimes
attack who they are, which is far more hurtful than
addressing a behavior or a choice. ~ Dr. Brené Brown

There is no need to be apologetic about *not* being able to be *everything* for *everyone* at *each* and *every time* that they request of you. You shouldn't put off your aspirations and goals for your life because you are appeasing others. You should not be their sole resource. You are not responsible for their life decisions. If they have repeatedly put themselves in less than favorable situations, it is their responsibility to fix it, not yours. Do not allow people to make you feel guilty because they accuse you of 'changing'. They want you to be responsible for their wants and needs because you are now successful or because you "made it out". Everyone has the *same 24 hours* in a day. The *same God* that blessed you, likewise, can bless them.

You are not obligated to do the work to build someone's else life. You will become an enabler if you do not allow them to take control over their circumstances. Break that dependency bond that they have developed. What would they do if you weren't in their life? How would they manage? *Exactly, they will figure it out.* Because by continually coming to the rescue, you do not give them the chance to take ownership and be accountable. Therefore, you are unwittingly contributing to the dismal, repetitive behavior that is continuously stunting their growth.

Setting boundaries is a way of caring for myself. It doesn't make me mean, selfish, or uncaring {just} because I don't do things your way. I care about me, too. ~ Christine Morgan

If applicable, analyze why you may feel compelled to permit lines to be blurred. If you can justify the *why* behind your actions of being a rescuer, it will motivate you to prioritize whom or what deserves your attention. By creating healthy boundaries, you are opening yourself up to more possibilities to expand upon your own passions and to pursue your purpose. You may reach a compromise but it should not be at the expense of jeopardizing your freedom, peace, obligations, finances, health, and/or happiness. Do not abandon your own objectives in an exchange to be popular, nice, or helpful. When you set restrictions, the people *that truly matter* will understand and respect those parameters.

Life is 10% what happens to you and 90% how you react to it. ~ Charles Swindoll

First and foremost, it is mandatory to make certain that you have made yourself a priority in your own life. Be mindful of how much you are willing to take. You must be specific about what you will or will not tolerate in your life. Be ready to affirm that it is non-negotiable. When you have established clear and definite standards, you will model how individuals should treat you. Your personal demonstration will resonate with others that they should be leery about being manipulative or attempting to take advantage of you. There should be something about your persona that conveys, *"I am not the one. Don't even try it."* By exhibiting the valuable characteristics of self-respect and self-worth, you avail yourself the autonomy to freely and genuinely love and to be loved by others.

Give and Receive Love

---

*It's not how much we give but how much love
we put into giving. ~ Mother Teresa*

Love is a huge, four-letter word that exudes so much confidence and power. Love can evoke such emotion that it can send an individual on the highest of highs or the lowest of lows. It can stop or start wars. Love has unequivocal healing powers. It has been observed that terminally ill patients may hold on just long enough, delay death, for a loved one to arrive by their bedside to say goodbye. The bond of love is so strong that it has been heavily speculated that when some individuals lose a loved one, they, too, may pass away. The cause of demise being ruled as a broken heart.

Love is potent. Love is a verb. Love in action is very influential and could change the entire course of your life. The very presence of love can motivate you to excel to heights that will display the very best version of yourself. Love can provide the fuel that you need to gain traction on a dream. Love is humbling and selfless. When you operate in love, you altruistically put others' needs and desires ahead of your own. You are unhesitant to make sacrifices. Despite any uncertainty, you remove the guard and become completely vulnerable. You readily share co-ownership of your heart with your significant other; you allow them to set up residency by offering up prime real estate space within your heart and mind. Even with the looming possibility of being heartbroken, it is a risk that many are eagerly willing to take a gamble on.

---

*Love makes your soul crawl out from its
hiding place. ~ Zora Neale Hurston*

Giving and receiving love engrains a credence within you and stimulates a courage that creates the notion that you can conquer *anything.* It energizes you; it can give you confidence. Especially when love is reciprocated, the feeling is indescribable. *(Note: Being deeply loved by someone gives you strength, while loving someone deeply gives you courage. ~ Lao Tzu)* Many individuals long for a divinely-aligned, loving union. Being opened to positive energy allows you to amplify your love, compassion, encouragement, understanding, consideration, forgiveness, and exhibit an acceptance of differences. A Harvard study has found it evident that the presence of love is the biggest indicator that contributes to a person's ability to cultivate a fulfilling life that exudes an abundance of happiness.

---

*Fall in love with someone who makes you
glad to be different. ~ Sue Zhao*

You do not score points nor should you keep tally marks of the numerous acts of love or the lack of affectionate gestures shown to one another. Real love will produce distinct, measurable evidence of how much you are investing in yourself and in your relationships. Love inspires you to consistently uplift, protect, and encourage each other. They are the first person you want to speak with when you receive good or bad news. The cadence of their voice and choice of words is calming and reassuring. They exhibit a pleasant tone. Conversations are not demeaning or condescending, but offers soothing comfort.

You both should be of one accord and equally-yoked because a house divided cannot stand. In a mutual partnership, you develop a pace and rhythm, like a well-choreographed dance. You openly communicate and are respectful of your companion's views. It is wonderful when not only do you love each other, but you also genuinely *like* one another. It is one thing to fall in love and *get* married *(wedding)*, but you must constantly put in the work *(marriage)* by pouring into your spouse, being attentive, faithful, and supportive. You should also maximize your efforts to *maintain* that sacred love to *stay* married. When properly cherished and nurtured, your love will grow. Periodically, it is natural to be attracted to someone, but *staying* in love is a *choice.*

And still, after all this time,
the Sun has never said to the Earth,
"You owe me."
Look what happens with love like that.
It lights up the sky. ~ Rumi

There can be times when love may go awry, but that should not diminish your hope and faith. Do not create a fortress of protection so secure that ultimately, the barrier designed to protect you from heartbreak, ultimately becomes a wall that keeps love out. Learn your lessons, but do not allow the lessons to inject so much fear that you remain isolated and never truly get to experience the exhilaration that real love can bring into your life. *To love and to be loved* is an opportunity to make wrongs, right; to be empathetic; to be protective; to be authentic.

Love is the only force capable of transforming an
enemy into a friend. ~ Dr. Martin Luther King, Jr.

Become awaken daily to explore an array of possibilities. Renounce any signs of apprehension and remove the shield that is guarding your heart. Do not allow past hurts to forfeit your chance to relish in the powerful, euphoric waves of uninhibited sensations that you could exclusively experience in this present moment, the *here and now.* Do not constantly be in a rush, slow down, and pause. Take a second to carefully look all around. Meticulously, scan the vicinity. Let the view slowly marinate into your consciousness. Upon close observation, you can find slivers of love everywhere. Love is completely surrounding you. *Can you see it? Do you feel it?*

Love is the bridge between you and everything. ~ Rumi

Now, identify at least one thing in your immediate proximity that you deem could be a representation of love. It can be any animate or inanimate object... What did you choose? Briefly, reflect on this selection and the feelings associated with your choice. Incorporate this daily exercise of intentionally seeking out subtle hints or examples that remind you of love. You will be astonished at the positive influence that this practice will have in your life. It can heighten your sense of awareness, create positive thoughts, invigorate and maximize your energy.

You have to learn to get up from the table, when love is no longer being served. ~ Nina Simone

Regrettably, at times there can also be a depressing and debilitating aspect to this intoxicating affection. As exhilarating and refreshing as love can be, by no means should you throw caution to the wind and disgrace yourself. Forgiveness does not set the precedent of accepting continual disloyalty or humiliation. Wanting to trust and believe in someone that you love should not negate from having common sense.

The worst loneliness is to not be comfortable with yourself. ~ Mark Twain

Do not allow your judgment to be clouded by confusing being single or alone with the fear of being lonely. There is a distinct difference between being *alone* and being *lonely*. In addition, please do not misconstrue *lust* for *love*. Refuse to be taken advantage of under a guise of romantic overtures. Be attentive to the signs that may reveal that someone that you care deeply about may not be honest or forthcoming with you. Do not allow yourself to be disrespected if they want to juggle you with someone else. Make the decision for them. Retain your power and immediately take yourself out of the equation. They do not have to choose you. *You* choose *you*.

> *You cannot invest into someone that you*
> *cannot trust. ~ Bishop T.D. Jakes*

Your due diligence is to pray before committing to a relationship. Before diving in, what does God say about this person? You can avoid a lot of mishaps by consulting God, *first*. Trust your gut; tap into your discernment. Do not continue to invest in someone or something and reap nothing in return. You should be able to find solace in your spouse/significant other. Love should not hurt nor make you feel devoid. Don't give someone so much power that you don't know how you should feel today until you know how they feel. You are not a puppet with someone else pulling the strings. You are too incredible to settle for rationed love. Remember, there should be a fair exchange. **Never, ever, ever settle for crumbs.** Never forget that **you** are the prize. True love is worth the wait.

> *If we really love ourselves, everything in*
> *our life works. ~ Louise Hay*

If warranted, your love can be incrementally allotted to certain individuals. Depending on your situation, it is definitely possible to love someone from a distance. Please know that tough love is still a form of love. It is up to you to make that decision. If possible, love beyond your capacity, but do not judge others for loving within the scope of their capabilities. It is unloving to expect others to adhere to imposed expectations that they are simply unable or unwilling to commit to.

Similarly, your love should not be contingent upon everything solely going your way, *all the time*. Be willing to compromise. Do not expect others to love you just as you are, but you are unwilling to accept and love them just as they are. Refuse to live in the space of immaturity by constantly nitpicking, finding and amplifying faults. Do not manipulate another's love for you by being conniving to get what you want. Do not withhold your love in anger. Even if you are hurt, you still should not hate. *Love should always be bigger than hate.* Regardless of the circumstances, wish love and happiness onto others.

And now these three remain: faith, hope and love. But
the greatest of these is love. ~ 1 Corinthians 13:13

Embodying love makes you transparent; it thoroughly exposes you. Never expect someone else to complete you nor should you have to complete someone else. That is too much power, pressure, and responsibility for someone to undertake. *Loving yourself* and *being whole* are two of the most treasured assets that you can bring into a relationship. *(Note: How you love yourself is how you teach others to love you. ~ Rupi Kaur)* Being open to the idea of love does not mean that you must be immaculate to give or receive love. It does not equate to perfecting a certain lifestyle before love is made available to you. There is no need to be hesitant to extend an invitation to welcome love. Nor should you stall the process when love does appear.

Design each day with an intention to love in an array of capacities. Jesus precisely models the epitome of what true love is when He gave His life for us. Be constantly reminded to love others as God loves us. His love safeguards us from any darkness. He does not keep score of our wrongdoings. The Lord's love is impeccable, invincible, and infallible. It is pure, forgiving, selfless, restorative, and uplifting. Pray for, protect, cover, and honor whom and what you love.

Anxiety in the heart of man causes depression, but
a good word makes it glad. ~ Proverbs 12:25

As Goethe shared, "*You can easily judge the character of a man by how he treats those who can do nothing for him.*" Be kind to each other. Believe in the goodness of people. Recognize that your words, acknowledgement, a hug or a simple smile can be a catalyst for change. Love one another. *(Note: Above all, love each other deeply, because love covers a multitude of sins. ~ 1 Peter 4:8)* When we live in a land of love, we realize that we are more alike than we are different. *You* are love and everything that it encompasses. When we practice unconditional love, we can uplift humanity. We become united, as *one entity.* And, it is within this unity, that we can potentially make a powerful difference, add value, and have a lasting, positive impact on the world.

Chapter II: Being Balanced
Self-Coaching Session

1. Have you ever forgotten to put yourself on your "To-Do" list? Please explain.

2. Are you a priority in your own life? Provide examples of how and when you have put yourself first?

3. In what way(s) can you start to show up for yourself and begin your journey to complete happiness?

4. Are there people or circumstances in your life that you feel are manipulative? Do you believe that you are being taken advantage of? How? List them.

5. In what area(s) of your life do you need to set boundaries? Please provide an in-depth response.

6. What resources do you need to help create a healthy balance in your life?

7. How do you express your love to others?

8. How can you daily incorporate love into your life?

Chapter II: Being Balanced
Self-Reflection Notes

_____

_____

_____

_____

_____

_____

_____

_____

_____

_____

_____

_____

_____

_____

_____

_____

Elevated BY
FAITH AND GRATITUDE

If the only prayer you ever say in your entire life is...
Thank You... it will be enough. ~ Meister Eckhart

When I Truly Began to Seek God, I Found Myself

When Thou said, seek ye My face; my heart said unto
Thee, Thy face, Lord, will I seek. ~ Psalm 27:8

Despite my previous peccadillos, I have been graciously forgiven. God is definitely taking me to new levels in Him. I am being stretched beyond and soaring to unprecedented heights. Although I am flawed, it does not encumber my personal qualities of being relatable, candid and transparent. I embody true character, integrity, tenacity, and I have the love of God in my life. Because I know *who* I am and *Whose* I am, my authenticity is one of my greatest assets. I am, without a doubt, unequivocally <u>still</u> a work-in-progress, but by seeking His face I know that all things work together for the good of those that love the Lord and are called according to His purpose.

The Lord is a refuge for the oppressed, a stronghold
in times of trouble. Those who know Your name
will trust in You, for You, Lord, have never
forsaken those who seek You. ~ Psalm 9:9-10

Our private historical archive stores a wealth of priceless information that justifies our current position and holds the blueprint to reassembling and renovating our life. I reevaluated my past experiences and attempted to make the necessary adjustments that were in alignment with my new mindset. I have created my own personal self-description about rediscovering and redefining myself. I am evolving into a woman that is fervently sold out for Jesus and truly lives for the Lord.

No matter how painful many of my mistakes were, I attempted to look at these trials and tests from a fresh perspective. I identified any repetitious behavior, evaluated my findings, harnessed the knowledge, and received guidance from the data. There is nothing new that hasn't already been. I constantly reflect, pray, meditate, study God's word, and believe what He says about me. The Lord is not a man that He should lie about anything that He ordains. It shall all come to pass; His word will not return void. I will always hold onto the Lord's truth throughout my journey. I do not know what the future holds, but I do know *Who* holds the future.

> *The thing that hath been, it is that which shall be; and*
> *that which is done is that which shall be done: and there*
> *is no new thing under the sun. ~ Ecclesiastes 1:9*

If we remain aloof of our negative patterns, it goes without saying, that those precedents can be the origin of our problems. When we are searching for our real identity, we must analyze our center/core and foundation. It gives the impression that we are on a scavenger hunt for clues and in a sense, we are. We almost have to be reintroduced to ourselves when we are in the process of becoming renewed. We must ensure that we are consistently examining and reexamining our efforts and making new revisions. During this course, take very careful measures to make choices that are conducive to your new mindset and journey. If you become tired or weary, God will provide you with the rest that you need to sustain you. The Lord is your safe place, your refuge. He is the shield that protects you. Stand on His word. When you are in alignment with the gifts that you possess *within* you, there will be no need to fear the obstacles that are surrounding you.

> *Sow to yourselves in righteousness, reap in mercy; break*
> *up your fallow ground: for it is time to seek the Lord, till*
> *He come and rain righteousness upon you. ~ Hosea 10:12*

We are so blessed to know that God is ordering our footsteps. We should yearn to fulfill His purpose, attain spiritual maturity, and become a living testimony. Remember that we have a God that sits high and looks low. His eye is always on us. Beloved, I encourage you to get to know Him. *(Note: I want to know Christ. ~ Philippians 3:10)* Wholeheartedly, seek the Lord's face; it will *literally* change your life. Jeremiah 29:13 declares that *"You will seek Me and find Me when you seek Me with all your heart."* Pray for an encounter with the Lord; He will stretch you and strengthen your faith. Nothing that you have gone through can keep you constrained any longer. Immerse yourself in pure mindfulness to become awaken and present in every moment. *You must begin to see yourself for the miracle that you are.* During this awakening process, you will find the validity and courage to be yourself. You can *be* everything that you seek, desire and admire.

Die to the past every moment. You don't need it.
Only refer to it when it is absolutely relevant to the
present. Feel the power of this moment and the fullness
of Being. Feel your presence. ~ Eckhart Tolle

Don't Give Up... God Hears You

Be still and know that I am God... ~ Psalm 46:10

Do not think that God has forsaken you in times of trouble, as a matter-of-fact, God hastens toward you in your time of need. God is protective and caring. His love and presence are constant. His eye is always on you. You are always within His reach. Sometimes it may appear that God does not hear you when you assume that He has allowed your prayers to go unanswered. But this is His way of getting your full attention. The Lord's strength is perfected in your weaknesses. He walks beside you so that you are not alone. And if you become too fatigued to amble along, He will carry you.

God is building your endurance while educating you through your experiences. Your newfound knowledge hones your skills and enhances your wisdom, patience, hope, and faith. Norman Vincent Peale would iterate, *"When God wants to send you a gift, He wraps it up in a problem. The bigger the gift that God wants to send you, the bigger the problem He wraps it up in."*

They that wait upon the Lord shall renew
their strength. ~ Isaiah 40:31

If our Heavenly Father takes care of the birds in the air, please know that He will take care of us. When we are impatient, we run the risk of ruining everything and encumbering the outcome to our circumstances. Because of our disobedience, distractions will occur to deter us from reaching our destination. For the record, the distractions are the feint of the enemy; so, that he can pilfer our focus and time. Remember, the enemy comes to kill, steal, and destroy. Postponing what God has instructed us to do, gives a foothold to the adversary. When we fall for his deceitfulness and shift our attention, we unnecessarily prolong our destiny.

I will refine them like silver and test them like gold. They will
call on My name and I will answer them. ~ Zechariah 13:9

By insisting on doing things our way, we forgo the Lord's instructions and begin to wander aimlessly without a sense of direction. It may take us 40 *years* to reach our goals, instead of the 3 *days* if we had only remained faithful and waited on the Lord. Never forget that we are not in control. **God is**. He may not come when we want Him to, but He is *always* right on time. God will bring His promises to pass. We are indebted to Him. We will never, ever be able to repay what God has done for us. He has kept us. His grace and mercy protect us. Never give up. *The Lord definitely hears you.*

Being confident of this very thing, that He which
hath begun a good work in you will perform it
until the day of Jesus Christ. ~ Philippians 1:6

Along your journey, you will encounter ups and downs. Do not falter when faced with the ebbs and flows of life. You must stay driven and steadfast. Be encouraged; remain faithful and patient. Continue *being* and *doing* your very best. Maintain your grit and composure. You cannot only believe in God when things are going the way that you would like, per your plans. You cannot solely have faith when the blessings are abounding. Your true character is revealed when times become rocky and tumultuous. Adversity brings to the forefront who you truly are.

The ultimate measure of a man {woman} is not
where he {she} stands in moments of comfort, but
where he {she} stands at times of challenge and
controversy. ~ Dr. Martin Luther King, Jr.

You shouldn't get frustrated when the deal falls through, or the relationship doesn't work out because that was the Lord's hand on it. He was redirecting you. Trust and be grateful for whatever God blocks because He is moving you out of harm's way. God is continuously thwarting attacks that you don't even know about. While you were sleeping, He was working things out on your behalf. *(Note: I believe that the attacks on your life have much more to do with who you might be in the future than who you have been in the past. ~ Lisa Bevere)* Don't ever feel that He has abandon you. God has a plan for your life.

Never give up on your dream... Perseverance is all important. If you don't have the desire and the belief in yourself to keep trying after you've been told you should quit, you'll never make it. ~ Tawni O'Dell

---

Every tongue that comes against you, He will hold in contempt. No weapon that comes against you shall prosper. Now, the Lord didn't say the weapons wouldn't form; He said that they wouldn't prosper. When God is for us, the *who's* don't even matter. Inferring from the scripture, Matthew 8:23-27, *when you lack faith and begin to have a conniption, He isn't worried. He is resting.* Viscerally, you should know that the Lord is covering you. Cease worrying. Don't doubt God. Stay faithful. Remain poised and graceful at all times. Your behavior is your best ministry.

And let us not be weary in well doing: for in due season we shall reap, if we faint not. ~ Galatians 6:9

The righteous cry out, and the Lord hears them; He delivers them from all their troubles. ~ Psalm 34:17 ~ Everything that you go through is God's preparation for you. God will take the very thing meant to break you and use it instead to bless you. He knows your beginning and your end. He knew you before you were formed in your mother's womb. Only He knows what is in store for you and your level of readiness to receive it.

And if ye have not been faithful in that
which is another man's, who shall give you
that which is your own? ~ Luke 16:12

You should never covet someone or something that belongs to someone else. *What is for you is for you.* Do not corrupt the gifts because you lust after things or people that are already attached. Even if you do acquire these forbidden fruit, so much trouble will most likely befall the situation, that you will be destined to lose them the same ill-gotten way that you obtained them.

We must be in earnest when we kneel at God's footstool.
Too often we get faint-hearted and quit praying at
the point when we ought to begin. We let go at the
very point where we should hold on strongest. Our
prayers are weak because they are not impassioned
by an unfailing and resistless will. ~ E.M. Bounds

If we receive our blessing too soon, it is a good chance that we may not be prepared for it. If we are ill-equipped to handle what God has in store for our lives, we could potentially become flummoxed by the responsibilities. If blessed prematurely, it would be reprehensible to mar or disavow the Lord's gifts to us.

It will behoove you to have patience and grow comfortable during the waiting phase, if not, you may block your blessings. *(Note: A little one shall become a thousand, and a small one a strong nation; I, the Lord, will hasten it in {the appointed} time. ~ Isaiah 60:22)* Whatever you don't face or acknowledge, you are susceptible to repeat. So, your past mistakes, troubling experiences, or lack of judgment are all key factors that will be used for creating a blank page upon which you can rewrite your story.

Don't you know that the day dawns after night,
showers displace drought, and spring and summer
follow winter? Then have hope! Hope forever, for
God will not fail you. ~ Charles Spurgeon

Look where God has brought you from. Those perceived setbacks were His inherent plan for ingeniously shaping, molding, nurturing, and edifying you. He is building a solid foundation of understanding through your trials and errors. So, that you can genuinely acquire the knowledge and wisdom that will then be utilized to give Him the glory by being a beloved proxy to serve others in His name. At the appropriate time, when you have sage and matured, He will answer you. Continue to be obedient and stay persistent. For it is by your unwavering faith that you will be led into a territory of, undeserved, abundance. In all things, put the Lord first. *(Note: But seek ye first the kingdom of God, and His righteousness; and all these things shall be added unto you. ~ Matthew 6:33)* Therefore, don't become weary. Keep working and seeking the kingdom of God. Your blessing is on the way. In due season, you will reap your harvest.

Do Not Miss God's Assignment

*Fear God, and keep His commandments: for this is the
whole duty of man. For God shall bring every work
into judgment, with every secret thing, whether it be
good, or whether it be evil. ~ Ecclesiastes 12: 13-14*

When we consistently obey the Lord's directions, we are adhering to God's expectations for us. We are sharpening our discernment as we prepare to embark upon a tedious expedition of self-exploration. It is imperative that we remain in compliance with the Lord's guidance as we traverse along unfamiliar trails. Uncertainty and confusion may seep in when we are not tenacious with our prayers. *(Note: You do not have, because you do not ask God. When you ask, you do not receive, because you ask with wrong motives. ~ James 4:2-3)* We should present our petitions with pure intentions and wait to receive His directives. Before we share our problems with anyone else, we should first take our concerns to God. Our most treasured communication should be a daily conversation with Him. Developing a relationship with the Lord is compulsory for our walk with Him.

*And whatsoever ye do, do it heartily, as to the Lord,
and not unto men; Knowing that of the Lord ye
shall receive the reward of the inheritance: for ye
serve the Lord Christ. ~ Colossians 3:23-24*

You were born for a specific reason. You are very fortunate to have an opportunity to create and live your legacy every single day. The Lord has placed a divine order on your life. When you are obedient and answer the call, your intentions effortlessly become in alignment with your vision. You begin to fulfill your mission. God's instructions are not always going to be big, blinking neon signs that will immediately grasp your attention. Sometimes, it is delivered in small increments. You must be cognizant of the smallest details. It may come as soft as a gentle whisper or as jarring as slamming into a brick wall. There should be a significant connection and completeness with your inner being. When you are attuned with your spirit, you will possess the proficiency to discern God's distinct voice and signs.

When a man's ways please the Lord, He maketh even
his enemies be at peace with him. ~ Proverbs 16:7

At times, you may become so engulfed in your roles and responsibilities, but this should not be an excuse to be negligent in the acknowledgment of your Creator. As a matter of fact, it would be remiss if you failed to do so. It is akin to receiving a present from an associate, never saying thank you, gushing over the tangible item, while completely ignoring your acquaintance. Not only would that be a display of rude and unacceptable behavior, it is also tacky and alludes to a lack of manners.

Be mindful of being attentive and tenacious. Our gratitude is emphasized when we praise and worship our Lord and Savior. Everything that we *are* and everything that we *have* is because *He is the Provider.* We should never be more enthralled with a gift, but instead give honor to the *Giver.* The *Giver* is the *Source* that has even more to give when we prove ourselves to be earnest. Our fidelity should not be exhibited because of what the Lord can *do* for us, but rather because of who He *is* to us.

I, the Lord, search all hearts and examine secret
motives. I give all people their due rewards, according
to what their actions deserve. ~ Jeremiah 17:10

God has examined your heart and mind. He knows everything about you. Regardless of your current situation, God is directly in the midst, with you at all times. He will give you a new heart and impart a new spirit within you to reaffirm your rebirth. The Lord's guiding word is a lamp unto your feet illumining your path. Listen intently to His commands and do not harden your heart. For it is God that wills and works within you to fulfill His divine purpose. When you follow God's precise orders for your life, He will give you the desires of your heart, but you must be prepared for what you have prayed for. And once you are prepared, *God will open doors that no man can shut.*

Be strong and courageous, and do the work. Do
not be afraid or discouraged, for the Lord God,
my God, is with you. ~ 1 Chronicles 28:20

Our assignment is why we are here. We should not get to the end of our lives and have not completed the tasks that we were created and equipped to perform. We are all uniquely and wonderfully made. *No one can do what each of us, individually, can do.* It was allocated, specifically, for us. When we put in the work, we prove ourselves to be trustworthy. To whom much is given, much is required. Being faithful over every big and small matter discloses that we are keenly listening to God's mandates. He responds by graciously granting our petitions. The ultimate goal is to hear our Lord say, *"Well done..."* Remain unshakable and boldly step into your assignment.

His Lord said unto him, Well done, thou good and
faithful servant: thou hast been faithful over a few
things, I will make thee ruler over many things: enter
thou into the joy of thy Lord. ~ Matthew 25:21

Release Fear and Embrace Faith

> *Take the first step in faith. You don't have
> to see the whole staircase. Just take the first
> step.* ~ Dr. Martin Luther King, Jr.

Deciding to step out on faith to pursue your passion is a choice that does not come without a deep pause. The thoughts of achieving any semblance of success are incredulous. Caught in the grips of fear, you feel partially paralyzed, frozen in time, unable to move. The silent hesitation can sound like bellowing echoes that meticulously tap dances on the faint strands of your weaken, nervous courage.

Somehow, you gather your wits and resolve that the rewards outweigh the risks. You decide to proceed on this purpose-filled excursion. Believing that your faith supersedes any cowardly anxiety, you invoke a sense of bravery to embark upon a journey that could forever change your life. In an intense search for your calling, you need clarity. Elicit your discernment to help guide you toward a sign… any sign that will confirm that you are on the right course.

> *Do not go where the path may lead, go instead where there
> is no path and leave a trail.* ~ Ralph Waldo Emerson

Have you ever been exposed to a new realization about yourself that you preferred to remain hidden? If only it were to lay dormant, you would be just fine with that. In our lucidness, we know that this isn't a reality. You must address it, regardless of how hard it may initially seem. Embarking upon the path to satisfy our continual quest for self-fulfillment, you may encounter many emotional hits and misses. The conclusion is that the challenges must stretch us to grow us. You will never know what you can overcome until you are faced with something that could potentially devastate you, but nevertheless, you will survive…

Trust in the Lord with all thine heart; and lean not unto thine own understanding. In all thy ways acknowledge Him, and He shall direct thy paths. ~ Proverbs 3:5-6

The ultimate value of this trek is the unveiling along the way. *What we learn about ourselves is the greatest benefit of all.* There will be remarkable discoveries, as well as some disappointments. In many instances, we may try to gloss over the inconvenient truths when we uncover something that we do not concur with or simply do not want to acknowledge, but eventually, we should concede that it is all a part of our growth; it's our story. Not settling for conformity, being a disruptor of the norm, can make you feel isolated. Sometimes to be exceptional and cutting-edge, you must *elevate* your vision. If you want to *standout*, initially, you may have to be willing to *stand alone.*

But by the grace of God I am what I am: and His grace which was bestowed upon me was not in vain; but I labored more abundantly than they all: yet not I, but the grace of God which was with me. ~ 1 Corinthians 15:10

There is no definite plan that precisely outlines your future. You must allow your consciousness to harness the flexibility to welcome uncertainty into the realm. Do not put on a masquerade depicting that you have it all together. It is time to put your ego in check. If you knew everything, where do you go from here? You will taint the opportunity to acquire more curiosity, wisdom, creativity, exploration, connections, and development. Please keep in mind, not all fear is bad. A healthy dose of fear is necessary; it keeps your instincts sharp and alerts you to any approaching dangers.

Cast all your anxiety on Him because He cares for you. ~ 1 Peter 5:7

I implore you to just ask and believe. Lay your troubles and concerns before God. The weight is too arduous for you to carry on your own. The logistics are not your concern. Attend to your *right now* and let the Lord take care of *the how*. Do not stress out about tomorrow, for it has its own troubles. Focus on the present and the belief that your crooked paths will be made straight. You will become like a tree that's planted by streams of living water. *(Note: Don't dig up in doubt what you planted in faith. ~ Elisabeth Elliot)* God has already ordained what is to transpire in your future seasons. Be obedient and trust that His will shall be done. Disregard the naysayers and doubters, but steadfastly trust in the Lord unconditionally with your whole heart and He will reward your obedience and faith in Him.

If you have faith and do not doubt... you can say to this mountain, 'Be thou removed, and be thou cast into the sea'; it shall be done. And all things, whatsoever ye shall ask in prayer, believing, ye shall receive. ~ Matthew 21:21-22

When we are vulnerable, we can admit that we do not know it all, but we are still willing to give it a try. Bouts of disbelief will attempt to seep in and try to sabotage your plans. Never let fear dictate your future. You must continue to believe even when the evidence appears to say otherwise. Whenever you feel dejected, Jesus is always right there with you, by your side. He will be whatever you need Him to be in that specific moment.

Even when you cannot track or trace God, you must still *trust* Him. He is reliable and will not disappoint you. Lift your hands in total praise, bow your head, abandon your fears, worship, and surrender it all to His will. There is an unspoken tranquil peace that envelops us when we submit ourselves and are guided by our intuition. This process can be extremely prophetic. So, do not be afraid to pursue the path that will unveil your true purpose. Where you start, is not where you have to finish.

Now faith is the substance of things hoped for, the
evidence of things not seen. ~ Hebrews 11:1

Fear can be scary; it may paralyze you. But, if you don't jump, you will never know what your life could be. You cannot be courageous and complacent simultaneously. You *must* believe, but most importantly, you must **do**. Faith without works is dead. Please do not let the enemy steal your curiosity. The tug that you feel within is a guiding compass that is either providing confirmation that you are exactly where you should be or gently urging you to change course. Faith raises your expectations. Don't settle for mediocrity by playing it safe because you are afraid of disappointment. Break your ritual of engaging in a monotonous routine. Proliferate productive patterns that will stretch you beyond your imagination.

Begin to live as though your prayers are
already answered. ~ Tony Robbins

Now, do not have the faith of a mustard seed and pray for your mountain to be removed or for the wall to come down, if you are not going to take advantage of the cleared path to chase your dreams. You must determine your next course of action. Live your life in such an honorable way that you are not petrified of dying. Death is a debt that we all must pay, but you should be deliberate about transitioning from the earthly to spiritual realm on *empty*. Do not die with your unrealized dreams still lingering inside of you.

Stop allowing pessimists, negativity, poseurs, or indecisiveness to interfere with you fulfilling your assignment. Do not be afraid to answer the call that is on your life. Fear can't stop want God wants to do in your life. God has already equipped you with the necessary tools that you need to kill your goliath. He is just summoning it to come forth. When you are obedient, you will seamlessly transform into whom and what you were always meant to be. In addition, you will reap the benefits that are afforded to you through the experience of not only being alive but most notably, the rewards of truly *living...*

Sometimes, You Have to Encourage Yourself

---

*And David was greatly distressed; but David encouraged
himself in the Lord his God. ~ 1 Samuel 30:6*

Inhale... Exhale, Inhale... Exhale, Inhale...Exhale... Take a moment to listen to your deep breaths as you breathe in… pause… and slowly release the air in your lungs. Do you hear that? The vibrations of the reverberating breaths as they flow in and out of your nostrils. Closing your eyes can further sensationalize this feeling and heighten your sense of awareness. Possessing the ability to breathe on your own and to feel the pulsating rhythm of your heartbeat is such a blessing that should not be taken for granted.

Each day is a miracle that is bestowed upon us; it is another chance to evolve. We are afforded an opportunity to be better than we were yesterday. Daily, we have the option to conduct a self-assessment that will prompt us to refocus, readjust, and reset our goals with a determination to *get it right*. Each attempt brings us closer than the last.

---

*A problem is a chance for you to do
your best. ~ Duke Ellington*

You must not lose sight of your goals. When challenges occur, they are not setbacks or stumbling blocks but consider them as stepping stones to navigate you closer to your purpose. Take any negative bricks being thrown at you and utilize them to build a solid foundation. Stay rooted in your faith. Do not become vexed or dismayed. Do not sway from your faith in Jesus Christ. Regardless of how daunting your situation may appear, stand flat-footed and never waver in your beliefs. Be brave. God's angels have a protective hedge around you.

*Be strong and courageous. Do not be terrified; do
not be discouraged, for the Lord your God will
be with you wherever you go. ~ Joshua 1:9*

What I feared has come upon me. ~ Job 3:25 ~ When you feel subjugated during your journey, take a moment for *'me-time'* to relax, release, rejuvenate, and become renewed. At some point, you should take a sabbatical so that you can take the necessary time to regroup, refresh, restore, and reevaluate your circumstances.

*Surely God is my salvation; I will trust and not be
afraid. The Lord, the Lord, is my strength and my
song; He has become my salvation. ~ Isaiah 12:2*

Refuse to become distracted by what your current situation looks like right now. You must not give up on yourself when things are not going the way that you initially planned. You must continue to *try, try, and try again.* Your efforts will not be in vain. To succeed, there is a formula. Hard work, determination, perseverance, and patience are significant elements for being successful. You are in a strategic partnership with God. *"With God"* all things are possible.

You are the epitome of what possibility looks like. You should be so driven by what you are believing God for that you refuse to let anyone or anything hinder what He has already predestined for your life. Allow the Lord to usher you into a new season and the next level of your life. Your dreams are not dead; they are just lying dormant. Stir up your passion, revive those visions, resuscitate your desires, ignite that flame, and go get your blessing.

*Cherish your visions and dreams as they are
the children of your soul, the blueprints of your
ultimate achievements. ~ Napoleon Hill*

Release any superficial timelines that you placed on your goals, reorganize, and *start now*. Don't concentrate only on the difficulties. Think about the circumstances that you once thought that you would not make it through, but you survived them, anyhow. There are lessons, blessings, and opportunities to be found in the adversities. Celebrate your triumphs. You are victorious. The Lord will prosper you. Always remember that you serve an almighty God that can dream a bigger dream for you than you could ever imagine.

Every great dream begins with a dreamer. Always remember, you have within you the strength, the patience, and the passion to reach for the stars to change the world. ~ Harriet Tubman

Please know that there is a very faint boundary between admiration and envy. Sometimes, individuals may become envious of you because they see your current status, but are unaware of your humble beginnings. They have no idea about all the combats and fiery blazes that you narrowly escaped. At times, the scorching flames were so close that the hairs on your arms were tinged. The smoke permeated your clothes and upon careful inspection, there's still a slight glimpse of smut smudged on your cheeks.

Anything can be assumed by looking at the exterior, but the Lord knows your heart. Those close calls and scars should not agonize you; they are esteemed badges that should be worn proudly. *You survived*. It is a reminder that no matter how difficult some circumstances *will* get, God is with you and you are going to make it.

We should always pray for help, but we should always listen for inspiration and impression to proceed in ways different from those we may have thought of. ~ John H. Groberg

Ask yourself the following self-assessment guiding questions and provide your responses in the *Self-Reflection Notes* section. Periodically, during various milestones in your life, review these questions and analyze if your responses have changed. This activity is a great resource that may help you to gauge your growth. A candid analysis of your daily schedules can assist with devising brilliant strategies that will help to evaluate and organize your priorities. You may have to be your own support system and cheerleader. *You are your own best asset and advocate.*

Self-Assessment Guiding Questions:

1. What are my strengths?

2. What are my weaknesses?

3. Am I fully committed to achieving my goals?

4. Am I engaging in productive activities that will produce a favorable outcome towards fulfilling my purpose?

5. Am I truly utilizing my full potential, faith, skills, and fostering relationships *(networking, mentors, coaches, continuously learning, following up, etc.)* to maximize God's plans for my life?

Don't be afraid of your fears. They are not there
to scare you. They're there to let you know that
something is worth it. ~ C. JoyBell C.

When you take an honest survey of your current life situation, you can determine what areas need improvement and consciously set your intentions to modify accordingly. Meditate on the revisions that will produce the greatest results and mood, then delve into the practice of self-renovation to formulate your vision. Disavow all negative outside influences. Concentrate on what would be an accurate depiction of your authentic identity. Remain steadfast to what resonates with you and how can you convey this perception to others. Be intentional about what you will authorize to be an authenticated representation of your best self.

You need people in your life who share your vision and have
good character. The people who influence you determine
who you become. Choose wisely. ~ Valorie Burton

Certain individuals may influence you, but the final decision is yours. Do not seek others' permission, endorsement or validation to live your best life. Characteristically, some people condemn what they don't understand. Every crass comment or criticism does not deserve your response. It is okay if others do not comprehend or appreciate your mission, drive, or ambition. *It is your vision, not theirs.* It is a good thing that your destiny isn't directly tied to them. Who is *them*? The first people that you immediately thought of while reading this passage.

Even though you couldn't quite put your finger on it, you have always discerned that something was amiss in your life. Your instinct magnified this unsettling inside of you, that there should be *something more*. At times, you have felt out of place, as if you didn't quite fit in or belong in certain circles. You were *with* the crowd, but you were not one *of* the crowd. You have always known that you are different. You think differently, speak differently, feel differently, act differently, and work differently. *(Note: You are on a different level.)* You realize that *you were created to make a positive difference.*

Everything that you are or will ever be is *already within* you. It is the very *center* of your being. You are empowered to do great and mighty things. *Never settle for being mediocre.* Refuse to be that person that does the bare minimum; only doing just enough to get by. You are too incredible and amazing to just be average. You are an articulate, precocious vessel. You are too blessed to live a "just good enough life." Speak over your life to evoke what you wish to be manifested. You have limitless abilities and you can *be, do,* and *have* whatever you choose. Open yourself up to a higher realm to receive boundless possibilities. Honor the greatness that is inside of you. Tap into the *core* of your own power.

What lies behind us and what lies before us are tiny matters compared to what lies within us. ~ Ralph Waldo Emerson

---

During the times that you may feel vanquished, take a deep breath, and encourage yourself. To get the jolt that you need to commence or continue your search, you may have to constantly stay motivated and remember your *why.* Sometimes it's your haters that will reveal how awesome you truly are. Ironically, it wasn't until they put the spotlight on you, by allowing their jealousy, immaturity, and insecurity to flare up, that you even began to comprehend the scope of your own strength and power. *(Note: Your greatness <u>should</u> make some individuals very uncomfortable; they may need to step up their own game. Do not be petty. Their offensives blatantly remind you of who and Whose you are.)* When you are under attack, it is because you possess something of value. The bigger the battle, the greater your victory. Be thankful for their unvarnished reminders and confirmation; it is just the push that you need to keep going.

Speak words of affirmation, prayer, and powerful mantras for motivation. This self-encouragement will inspire you to garner more strength and instill the desire within to continue to strive forward toward your goals. There is no need for trepidation when you are entrusted with a potentially revolutionary idea, a ground-breaking seed. At times, you may have to be *out-of-order*. You may have to be willing to be radical. Think outside of the box and be innovative. Embrace the unexpected.

The {woman} who has no imagination,
has no wings. ~ Muhammad Ali

Be inattentive to what is going *around* you, but instead concentrate on what is going on *within* you. Resist the temptation to fade into conventionality. Stimulate those inner stirrings to initiate change. *You* are a change agent. *You* are a catalyst for change. Successful people are pioneers. They operate differently, which is an asset that contributes to their success. You cannot wait for someone else to catch up to your vision or to get on board. You are an eagle and therefore, to ascend to new heights, you may have to fly solo. As a matter-of-fact, you can do some of your best work without the disruptions from others. You don't have time to explain every decision or move that you make; you are on a mission. (*Note: Eagles do not associate with crows or chickens; they thrive and fly with other eagles. And at all cost, they avoid vultures.*)

There is no greater agony than bearing an untold
story inside of you. ~ Dr. Maya Angelou

Your voice is a trumpet; make a joyful noise unto the Lord. Your tongue is likened to a pen of a ready writer. You have a good heart. You are a transformational leader and an influencer. You are blessed and highly favored. You do not know why God has chosen you, but He did, and therefore, He has qualified you. Your gifts will make room for you. (*Note: You are the gift.*)

God will strengthen, upgrade, and multiply your efforts. Only God can give the increase. Every endeavor and initiative that you begin will fall under God's anointing and protection. Always remember that you are the salt of the earth. You are boldly empowered. You are worthy. You are tenacious. You deserve to *be* the very best version of your authentic self and to live your best life. Rest in the assurance that your hard work will yield favorable results.

You are the light of the world. A town built on a hill cannot be hidden...In the same way, let your light shine before others, that they may see your good deeds and glorify your Father in heaven. ~ Matthew 5:14

The Importance of Gratitude

I have learnt to be content whatever the circumstances.
I know what it is to be in need, and I know what
it is to have plenty. ~ Philippians 4:11-12

When you are grateful for what you have, you open yourself up to *receive more* and to *become more*... Always be grateful for everything. The very things that we often take for granted, are some of the very things that someone else may be praying for. God will not promote us to the next level until we have proven ourselves efficient and appreciative for where we are currently positioned.

As previously mentioned, do not covet what does not belong to you. *What is for you, is for you.* When you focus on someone's else life, you may stall in your own race. Do not miss God's assignment by becoming distracted. Cultivate the memorable moments. You attract more goodness into your life when you value what you already possess. An insightful adage asserts that *"what you appreciate, appreciates."*

Enjoy the little things, for one day you may look back
and realize they were the big things. ~ Robert Breault

Count your blessings. There is always something or someone that you could be grateful for. Let's start with the fact that you woke up this morning. There is a cemetery full of people that would probably love to trade places with you right now for that reason alone. Each day is another chance or opportunity to *do* more and to *become* more. Before you ever throw yourself a pity-party, take a moment to find someone else that you can bless. In the divine spirit of giving, which is such an expressive gesture, you will uplift your own countenance. Be happy for others. Cherish the simple joy of being a giver. Add a little magic to someone else's life and your life will become enriched and blessed, as well.

This is the day that the Lord has made; Let us
rejoice and be glad in it. ~ Psalm 118:24

Being continuously thankful is not always an easy feat. You may find it easier to complain about what you don't have instead of valuing what you do have. Lack can make you become unreceptive and unappreciative. Although it can prove to be challenging to say, 'Thank You' during taxing situations, you should extend thanks, anyway. Understandably, sometimes things will go wrong in your life, but you should always remember that God can change your circumstances in an instant. He can give you light in place of darkness, hope from despair, peace from pieces. It is so important to be thankful. The greater your gratitude, the more the universe will open up and reveal its hidden treasures and many, astounding wonders to you. Life really wants the best for you. Release any toxicity that threatens to derail your health and happiness. Open yourself up to make room for God's goodness to be poured into you.

The unthankful heart discovers no mercies; but
the thankful heart will find, in every hour, some
heavenly blessings. ~ Henry Ward Beecher

If there is a constant barge of grievances that take precedent in your life, then the grass will always appear greener on the other side. *(Note: It's hard to be hateful when you are grateful. ~ Chris Hogan)* Let me attest that if you water your own grass, spray the weeds, add topsoil, and plant a few flowers… the landscape of your lawn will look just as attractive. And for all that you know, the grass 'on the other side' could be fake, turf grass.

In everything give thanks; for this is God's will for
you in Christ Jesus. ~ 1 Thessalonians 5:18

You must be confident and believe that even though the circumstances may become perplexing and difficult, God has provided you with the fortitude to get through any privation. Do you really believe that He would have brought you through everything that you survived, only to abandon you now? *You've come too far by faith for this to be all that there is.* You are not done; there is so much more for you to do. You are skillfully equipped with forte and self-preservation. Gratitude affords you the grace to transform your mentality, which can ultimately transition a negative experience into a positive lesson. Be mindful of not making a permanent decision out of a temporary situation. *This, too, shall pass...*

Gratitude is the fairest blossom which springs
from the soul. ~ Henry Ward Beecher

Dwell in the land of compassion and appreciation. When you focus on what is good, you invite more of this goodness into your space, which, therefore, will expand your territory. When you show gratitude for what you have, you open yourself up to receive an influx of happiness, clarity, harmony, grace, constancy, and increase. Each day affords you an opportunity to discover tremendous possibilities, to learn new things, and to live more fully. There is always, always something to be grateful for. The Lord will guard your inheritance and cause your cup of blessings to overflow. You will always *be* and *have* more than enough. Your persona will virtually radiate the serenity that anchors your inner peace.

As we express our gratitude, we must never forget
that the highest appreciation is not to utter words
but to live by them. ~ John F. Kennedy

Express gratitude for what you have. Savor life's precious moments. Show the people that are important to you, how much you love and value them. I am appreciative of my mother, *GG*. She imparted subtle life lessons with levity, in her firm and unique style. I am thankful for my many family members, friends, and others, that were a part of or contributed to specific seasons. Your prayers and significant roles (*whether positive or negative*) over the course of my entire life has made such a tremendous impression on who I am today. Most particularly, I am sincerely grateful for my late *Aunt Caroline*, whose kind heart, support, and beyond caring for me as her niece, but truly loving me as a daughter, was so impactful.

Gratitude turns what we have into enough, and more. It
turns denial into acceptance, chaos into order, confusion
into clarity... it makes sense of our past, brings peace for
today, and creates a vision for tomorrow. ~ Melody Beattie

Studies have shown that gratitude is a proven stress reliever, which has beneficial effects on your heart, blood pressure, and ultimately, the longevity of your life. Create a *Gratitude* journal and reflect on at least three things each day that you are grateful for and write them down. This documentation can assist with alleviating numerous stressors in your life and gently remind you of what is truly important. Make a commitment to ensure that showing gratitude becomes a daily habit.

Chapter III: Faith and Gratitude
Self-Coaching Session

1. Have you ever wanted to give up on someone or something? Please explain.

2. Does it seem that, at times, the Lord does not hear your prayers? What requests have you submitted to the Lord that you believe He has not answered, yet?

3. Have you persevered despite facing obstacles or challenges? How did your faith help to sustain you?

4. In what area(s) of your life do you need to release fear and embrace faith?

5. In what way(s) do you believe that you are fulfilling your calling?

6. Who or what are you thankful for? Why?

7. In what way(s) do you practice gratitude? Please be specific.

8. Have you ever felt the need to seek validation from others? Please explain.

9. Do you feel that you always need someone else to motivate you to follow your dreams? Why or Why not?

10. Has anyone ever tried to convince you that it is not a good idea to pursue your passion? How have they tried to talk you out of following your dreams? How did you respond? Please be specific.

11. Please share whom you consider to be a worthy role model to emulate. What characteristics do they exhibit?

12. Do you realize that you should be your 'biggest cheerleader', that you are your own best advocate? In what area(s) can you encourage yourself to continue to strive for excellence?

13. Identify specific strategies that you can implement to improve your current circumstances.

Chapter III: Faith and Gratitude
Self-Reflection Notes

CHAPTER IV

Elevated BY
BEING EMPOWERED

> *We all make mistakes, have struggles, and even regret things in our past. But you are not your mistakes, you are not your struggles, and you are here NOW with the power to shape your day and your future.* ~ Dr. Steve Maraboli

Reclaim Your Power

*The most common way people give up their power is
by thinking they don't have any. ~ Alice Walker*

To reclaim your power, you may need to change your perspective. Your mindset needs to shift to redirect your energies toward acquiescing an alternate outcome for your life. You cannot control all the circumstances that will occur in your life, but you can be open and flexible enough that the difficult times do not have the permanent authority to negatively shape the overall evolution of your existence.

*Women have to harness their power; it's absolutely true.
It's just learning not to take the first no. And if you can't
go straight ahead, you go around the corner. ~ Cher*

Do not become so intimidated that you retreat into the 'familiar' arms of conformism. The very successful and powerful know that it takes *audaciousness* and a *strong belief in self* to accomplish your goals. The most important step is to simply *begin*. To get to where you want to go, you must begin where you are. You cannot proficiently accomplish a goal that you do not set. Learn to let your work speak for itself. When you are secure, you can move in silence. To be the most productive and effective, always *speak less, listen more, and be very observant.*

*A woman is the full circle. Within her is the power to
create, nurture and transform. ~ Diane Mariechild*

Do not give fear the permission to become bigger than your heart, drive, desire, bravery, or vulnerability. Go after what you want and take hold of it. If you want to truly reclaim your power, you must not, under any undue circumstances, settle for being mundane or mediocre. No one should ever strive to be basic. You should not be content with just blending in or fading into obscurity. Don't swindle yourself out of copious opportunities to be unique and unorthodox because you are too diffident to go after what you truly desire. If God gave you the vision, He also fortified you with what you need to see it through. Believe in yourself. You are endowed with God's abundant promises and provisions for your life.

Believe you can and you're halfway
there. ~Theodore Roosevelt

Dismiss the temptation to have a defeatist attitude. No matter how long it may take or how difficult it may become, *do not quit.* Your vision and determination are the required cogs needed to initiate the appropriate actions to live your best life; an empowered life. Do not resort to being supercilious and getting caught up on a timeline. Do not rush and make careless, avoidable mistakes. Be very strategic because it is during this developing process that valuable knowledge and growth are obtained. What you glean along the way is instrumental. It will provide the sagacity to help you *maintain* the status once it is attained.

Reality can be shaped and changed by my direct actions, and
so I will act with constancy to forge my ideal life. ~ Unknown

To make significant strides and advance in your life, you should feel compelled to take immediate action. There must be a sense of urgency to get started truly living your life and not allowing life to simply just happen to you. You can't afford to keep wasting time. Hours turn into days, days turn into weeks, weeks turn into months, and months turn into years. And before you know it, you will look up and not be able to fathom what happened. Where did the time go? Be intentional about your daily decisions and take responsibility for the outcomes.

Plans are only good intentions unless they immediately degenerate into hard work. ~ Peter Drucker

---

Your purpose and power will be measured by your actions, not your intentions. Now, please do not get me wrong; I am an advocate of *setting your intentions.* You need to devise an efficient strategy to adopt the best practices to bring your intentions into manifestation. Position yourself to determine how you would like to be defined. It is not only critical that you *want* it, but the real powerful, transformational key is that you must *become* it.

Nothing external to you has any power over you. Ralph Waldo Emerson

---

The essential elements of owning your power are to consistently connect, grow, contribute, love, show respect, evolve and make progress. Each day is an opportunity to work on yourself to become better than you were the day before. *You have everything that you need within you.* You are emphatically empowered to birth your dreams into existence. Tap into your potential and activate your power and prosper. If you need to refocus, please do so. Pivot, if necessary. Always remember that while you are taking ownership of your appointed position, please ensure that you maintain your integrity as you advance.

Stand up straight and realize who you are, that you
tower over your circumstances. ~ Dr. Maya Angelou

Do not become stationary, putting your life on hold, waiting for someone to substantiate you. If necessary, affirm and endorse yourself. You cannot allow others' opinions or censure of you to determine your future. *Hateration* is simply confirmation that you are on the right path. Decide what you want. Your resolutions will incite self-assurance and serve as a blueprint to renovate your life. Your own beliefs and your heart's desires are what you should sincerely care about. Eventually, it is all that truthfully matters.

You've always had the power, my dear. You just had to learn
it for yourself. ~ Glinda, the Good Witch, Wizard of Oz

You must be confident enough to have tenacious faith to design the type of life that you want to live. Inevitably, there will be moments of doubt and uncertainty, but this is to be expected. These moments of disbelief are fleeting. The road to greatness is never found along a straight path; there will be many curves, twists and turns, but you must stay the course. At some point during your journey, the scenery could start to look familiar. You will have a nostalgic moment of déjà vu. You may even exclaim that *"I have been here before"*. There is no new thing under the sun. Continue this trek of self-discovery until you come full-circle. Your ending will always be better than your beginning. Your latter days will be greater than your former days.

We shall not cease from exploration And the end of
all our exploring Will be to arrive where we started
And know the place for the first time. ~ T.S. Eliot

Embracing the Power of "No"

> We need to find the courage to say NO to the
> things and people that are not serving us if we
> want to rediscover ourselves and live our lives
> with authenticity. ~ Barbara de Angelis

Have you ever felt even the slightest tinge of guilt for saying *"No"*? Do you incessantly beat yourself up because you are afraid of disappointing others? Does your *"Yes"* come with contingencies? Have you committed to so many *"Yeses"* that your life is spiraling out-of-control because it is constantly in a state of hysterics from engaging in a frenzied lifestyle? Are you seeking approval or wanting to ensure that you are liked by others? What you must remember is that when you are doing so much for everyone else, while not taking care of yourself that is considered as self-sabotage. To maintain a healthy balance in your own life, you need to create boundaries. You must personify your expectations.

> Example is not the main thing in influencing
> others. It is the only thing. ~ Albert Schweitzer

Typically, the word, *"No"* is associated with the terms: negativity, rejection, denial, rudeness, being inconsiderate, or insensitive. But depending upon the circumstances, the word, *"No"*, can be very empowering and liberating. It gives you the authority to be selective about the important opportunities that deserve your *"Yes"*. Your decision *not to do* something is just as prevalent as what you decide *to do*.

> There is nothing more powerful than a
> made-up mind. ~ Lewis Gordon Pugh

By the same token, likewise, being told *"No"* can also be redemptive. It authorizes you to refocus, recalibrate, reroute, and deposit your energy toward a new direction. It frees you from any false expectations and inhibitions. It releases you from being phony and performing under a façade. You must differentiate yourself from the comfort and commonality of always blending in.

I am thankful for all of those who said No to me. It's because of them that I did it myself. ~ Albert Einstein

Recognizing that you do not need to seek others' approval or validation empowers you to depend upon God and yourself. You can literally stimulate your growth when you release negativity. If you repetitively hear a *"yes"* response all the time, you will never be challenged. When you confidently address and overcome obstacles, you are *elevated* in unfathomable ways that will stretch you beyond your imagination.

Remember that not getting what you want is sometimes a wonderful stroke of luck. ~ The Dalai Lama

In some cases, you need to be grateful for the doors that *did not* open. *"No"* can also set you on a path to discover what you are really made of. Are you persistent, driven, ambitious, or motivated enough to continue to pursue your aspirations? Never give up on your dreams, regardless of what anyone tells you or even what you may say to yourself, sometimes.

Every *"No"*, brings you closer to your *Yes… You only need one Yes.* You are nurturing a persona that fosters self-respect. Your resilience is a mirror that models how people should treat you. Contrary to some popular beliefs, hearing *"No"* does not have to be the end of your story. It does not give you permission to give up nor does saying *"No"* make you a bad person. In many instances, it can awaken and rejuvenate a wonderful, new beginning for you.

*People think focus means saying yes to the thing you've got
to focus on. But that's not what it means at all. It means
saying No to the hundred other good ideas that there are.
You have to pick carefully. I'm actually as proud of the things
we haven't done as the things we have done. ~ Steve Jobs*

10 Positive Benefits of Utilizing and Embracing the Word "NO":

1. It helps you to alleviate unnecessary stress in your life.
2. It releases you from fear.
3. You will possess ownership over your choices.
4. It creates or reestablishes your confidence and gives you a renewed sense of self-worth.
5. It frees you to prioritize and value what is important to you.
6. It will enhance your ability to be decisive and effective.
7. The word, *"No"*, can spark and promote your growth and creativity as an individual.
8. It can encourage you to re-evaluate and re-assess situations and make pertinent changes.
9. It can also motivate you to negate from any notions of regret.
10. It does not hold you hostage to commitments that you wish you had never agreed to in the first place. Time is valuable; *"No"* can help you to clear your schedule.

The Gift of Goodbye

---

*If you're brave enough to say goodbye, life will
reward you with a new hello. ~ Paulo Coelho*

Everyone goes through *'growing pains'*. Learning to let go of those things that are no longer beneficial for your advancement is a sign of maturity. These transitions are necessary to stretch you and to stimulate your growth. When you are continually being expanded, it is natural to *outgrow* situations, things, and people. If you are committed to making progress, you must be intentional about *not* remaining stagnant. Growth is a natural form of evolving; it signifies life. Nothing should remain the same. The landscape of your life *should* begin to look differently as you continuously make strides and progressions. You must purge the inessentials. Don't look backwards. *(Note: There are far, far better things ahead than any we leave behind. ~ C.S. Lewis)* Learn to let go and trust what lies ahead.

---

*If I get stuck in who I am now, I will never blossom
into who I might become. I need to practice
the gentle art of letting go. ~ Sam Keen*

Do not bother with having feelings of regret. All experiences and relationships were necessary to help develop you into the person that you are today. Self-development is critically vital to becoming a better version of yourself. The dilemmas were resource tools used to enlighten you about what you should or should not do. *(Note: Maybe one day we shall be glad to remember even these hardships. ~ Virgil)* Not all burdens are created equally. Some troubles were designed to strengthen you, provide you with endurance, and to impart wisdom.

Embrace those precarious interactions that uplifted you for specific reasons and seasons, then move beyond the rest. Refuse to perpetuate the stress that worrying can generate. In due time, those superfluous concerns will subside. It may take facing trials and tribulations to recognize how strong you really are. When you are left with no other choice, you will definitely rise to the occasion.

When I was a child, I spoke as a child, I understood as a child, I thought as a child: but when I became a man {woman}, I put away childish things. ~ 1 Corinthians 13:11

It has often been conversed that when certain people enter our lives, it is for a *"reason or a season."* Some encounters are placed on our paths by divine appointment. We must champion our way through the assigned hardships to be given the authorization by God to proceed to the next level. When we have these connections, we should acknowledge them. And when they run their course and have come to a completion, we must let them go. *(Note: Have anyone ever left you too soon? They may have felt that they had gotten the best that you had to offer. They didn't realize that the best was yet to come. Do not beg them to stay; it's time to say, goodbye. It is imperative that you move on with your life.)*

Some circumstances occur to help cultivate your faith. When the mission is finalized, you would have proven yourself to be better, wiser, and stronger. If you do not successfully complete the task, you will continually repeat the course. Before being promoted to the next juncture in your life, you must be efficacious at your current level. So, if the situation or relationship does come to an end, do not become sad or mourn. It was only fated to last for a season. *(Note: The bonus benefit of implementing the gift of goodbye is that you inherit the gift of growth and begin to enlarge your capacity to 'glow up'.)* Letting go gives you permission to *be true to* yourself and to *be more of* your best self.

Many have become my enemies without cause; those who hate me without reason are numerous. ~ Psalm 38:19

Do not share your intentions with just anyone because not all people are trustworthy. Be very selective. Always remember that not everyone has your greater good in mind. Therefore, you must be cautious regarding your choice of confidantes. Many individuals will deceptively appear to admire you, but secretly resent your accomplishments and success. Ensure that your cohorts are the wind beneath your wings because they truly believe in you. They are there throughout the process of the struggles and hard work, and are not only present just to reap the rewards. They support you, not because of what you can *do* for them, but for *who you are.*

Your community of supporters should be your, *ride or die,* partners. They are your team. They are not judgmental or constantly holding you to your past mistakes. They do not set up roadblocks to detour you from your destiny. Utilize your discernment. Possess a keen sense of self-awareness, if not, you may inadvertently invite a lack of respect and disappointment into your life. Free yourself from anyone or anything that causes you any type of discomfort. It is imperative that you refrain from focusing on the negative, but instead concentrate on the wisdom that you gleaned because of the interaction or relationship. Many of your experiences occur to reveal to you what you *do not want* to have in your life. Each pivotal experience serves a specific purpose.

Learn to get in touch with the silence within
yourself and know that everything in life has
a purpose. ~ Elisabeth Kübler-Ross

We must pray and ask God for His guidance and impartation. It is in our stillness and mindfulness that we are replenished. Our lucidity will supersede any hint of ambiguity. God will allow what is necessary for progression to happen in our lives. The lessons provide us with the skills, maturity and knowledge, that will sharpen our discernment. Always, be grateful for everything because it has all been educational. Specific relationships are developed to be maintained for extended periods of time. If these associations end, it is okay. They were not *meant* to last forever. God places some people along our path to enhance our experiences and promote our opportunities to advance in different capacities or circumstances.

Don't chase people. Be yourself, do your own thing and work hard. The right people, the ones who really belong in your life, will come to you... and stay. ~ Will Smith

---

Only seek what is good and purposeful in those associations. If someone leaves or you must let them go, send them away joyfully. *Yes, joyfully; you should be jubilant.* Do not attempt restoration. Everyone that is currently in your life is not intended to go with you to the next level. *(Note: Just because some individuals may be in your present life or a part of your history that does not automatically qualify them to be a part of your future/destiny.)* Recognize that they played a key role in your life that has brought you closer to your purpose. It will all work together for your good. Utilize the *gift of goodbye* and release situations, items, positions, locations, and/or faux friends that are no longer beneficial or relevant for your evolution and escalation.

Don't let people who don't matter too much... matter too much. ~ Wes Moore

---

When you say *goodbye* to unproductive issues, you are free to receive, nourish, enhance, and focus on things that will make you better. When you are intentional about what deserves your attention and energy, you are more inclined to let go of things that have become a hindrance. No longer waste your time on irrelevant and insignificant matters. You can soar so much higher when you release the anchors of unnecessary people or issues that are weighing you down. You must say goodbye to some individuals when *helping* them results in *hurting* you. *(Note: Do not consent to being on 'lease' to someone and lose yourself in the process.)* You are responsible for the type of dynamics that you allow into your life. Cleanse your space. When you decide to release the people or situations that no longer serve an adequate purpose, God will provide the replacements that will have a much greater value. Trust God.

Make sure that nobody pays back wrong for wrong, but always try to be kind to each other and to everyone else. ~ 1 Thessalonians 5:15

Regardless, of the origin of the demise, exit the relationship with a level of grace, dignity, and class. Forgo the temptation to be vindictive. You are too blessed to hold a grudge. When you are a person of integrity, God will take care of any vengeance or retaliations. Always attempt to be a peacemaker. Ensure that you add value to all your involvements. Make it a goal to leave the partnerships better than how you found it. You can confidently hold your head up high when your conscience is clear and your departure does not comprise any lingering animosity. You do not have to necessarily 'forgive and forget'. At times, you may need to '*forgive and remember*', so that you do not get distracted from your purpose. It is vital that you are not prone to repetitively incur the same mistakes. Some lessons are too expensive to repeat and you cannot afford to constantly learn them over and over again.

You can't afford to be bitter. God may use the very people who cursed you, to bless you in the end. ~ Bishop T.D. Jakes

Self-evaluations must be conducted to gauge what is important in your life. Whoever or whatever that does not serve a distinct role that is productive for your destiny, you must make an executive decision and begin or complete the elimination process in your life. Loyalty and consistency are so very important. When you let go of whom or what you no longer need, the incentive is that you open yourself up to evolve, grow, and to be transformed. You will be able to determine how far you have come by deciphering that old situations no longer rile you. Those past matters are insignificant; you have moved beyond them. You are completely unbothered.

Sometimes something good has to be subtracted from our lives before something better can take its place. ~ Ann Spangler

---

Take a candid assessment of not only the people in your life, but also determine if you need to say goodbye to an area. It may be essential that you change your environment. You may be doing the *right thing* during the *right time*, but it *may not be at the right place*. Do not settle for feeling insignificant or small in a particular space. If your surroundings are holding you back, move forward to an environment in which you can thrive and be successful. Be prepared to relinquish whomever or whatever that may be keeping you from excelling to your greatest apexes. Always remember, that if doesn't *elevate*, then it is time for you to *eliminate*.

Obtain and Maintain a Positive Mindset

And be not conformed to this world: but be ye transformed
by the renewing of your mind. ~ Romans 12:2

You must become your biggest fan, your biggest cheerleader. *You* are your own #1 advocate. It is important to have a candid conversation with yourself daily. Your perspective is key to having a sanguine outlook on life. By nurturing your self-perceptions and attitude, you harness the skills to elevate your altitude. Your optimistic approach to life creates such a high-frequency that will automatically attract great things to you. There is no limit to what you can accomplish. Always remember that it is not about what happens to you, but your reaction to what happens to you. Regardless of the circumstances, you have a choice whether to respond in an optimistic manner. Take every negative thought into captivity. Do not permit toxicity to penetrate and contaminate your mind. Embody the temperament of only being positive and progressive. Your views can have a tremendous impact on your character, emotions, career, relationships, and/or environment.

To be resilient, you must take control of your thoughts
in the face of stress and challenges. If your thoughts are
counterproductive, change them. It takes practice, but
when you change what you say to yourself, you'll change
how you feel and what you do. ~ Valorie Burton

It is imperative to foster a setting that is conducive for positivity. Surround yourself with constructive and productive individuals that complement your work ethic and professional acumen. It is not about being competitive. You can collaborate and glean from their personal and world viewpoints. Everyone should be elated about affirming and encouraging one another. Go where you are loved, celebrated, and uplifted. The members of your inner circle should be the equivalent to a gathering of a mastermind group. Who is in your sphere of influence?

Ensure that you can delineate between the people who really have your back and those who only have your face. The difference is that the ones that have your back will stand in the gap and are loyal in and out of your presence. They are genuine, truthful, and may serve as your advisors or advocates. They are true champions of your vision.

Those that have your face are only supportive when they know that you are looking. Are they *helpers* or *haters* in disguise? They put on a full performance when they are aware that you are being attentive. You may need to take attendance because they will abandon you and are absent during the struggles, but they want to be present for the successes and celebrations. These facers or imposters will be revealed for who they truly are and should be dismissed immediately from being a part of your overflow season. Do not take it personal if you must block or delete someone from your rollcall. Desist from becoming upset or angry, simply evoke the *gift of goodbye*.

> *When you stop seeing others as rivals, you will celebrate who they are rather than envy them.* ~ Lisa Bevere

Do not be faithful and loyal to circumstances or individuals that are indifferent to you. Be mindful of making someone a priority in your life when you are only an option in theirs. No one values anything that is not perceived to be valuable. If they don't have any skin in the game, haven't made any sacrifices, or have an invested interest, they may feel entitled to be passive. You can identify these individuals by their lack of efforts or contributions to your relationship. They should truly care about what is happening to you, but instead they are indifferent. Despite what someone may *say*, what people *do* will show you *who they are*.

Differentiate between those that *undergird* you and those that *underestimate* you. Do they *support* you or want to *sabotage* you? Are they *empathetic* or are they *envious*? Are they *winners* or *whiners*? Are they *protectors* or *pretenders*? Are they *adding* to your life or *subtracting*? Are they *contributors* or *contaminators*? Are they sincerely *helpful* or *have hidden agendas*? Is their presence in your life, detrimental to your physical, mental, emotional, or financial wellbeing?

Your quality of life relies heavily upon your perceptions. Change your thinking, embrace your power, release some people, and shift into the position that God has already prepared for you. In the process, ensure that you do not forsake your dignity and veracity, but allow your honorable character to accurately represent who you truly are.

You should never share your problems with others because 80% of people don't care anyway, and the other 20% are kind of glad that you got them in the first place. ~ Ed Foreman

The most effective option is to tackle any obstacles to the best of your ability. Do not consent to bitterness taking root into your being. Staunchly resist allowing unwarranted privations to foil your mission. It is essential that you do not shrivel into stagnation when faced with a series of challenges. You do not need to announce every problem or struggle to an audience. Some issues should remain private because not everyone is going to be truthfully supportive. Stay motivated, persistent, discreet, and keep moving forward.

As a man thinketh in his heart, so is he. ~ Proverbs 23:7

Keep yourself in a land of gratitude. If you concentrate on what you are grateful for, even the smallest details, you will become receptive to being more appreciative and less inclined to complain. When you are less resistant, you are less likely to create negative emotions. When you realize that any situation could potentially be worse, you can pivot your thinking. You can shift the paradigm into feelings of gratitude. Protect your thoughts. Your thoughts are extremely powerful; they will either attract or repel what you want to manifest in your life. Meditate on magnetizing a calming and peaceful ambiance into your immediate environment.

*If you don't like something, change it; if you can't change
it, change the way you think about it. ~ Mary Engelbreit*

Typically, when individuals employ a positive mindset, they tend to excel in every area of their lives. They embody positive characteristics and will always find a silver lining in any situation. There is always an *opportunity beyond the obstacle*. There is no such thing as failure if you fail forward. You should not feel anguish if you can learn something redeemable in the process. The lesson is simply tutelage to gain perspicacity from the encounter. Our experiences help to shape and define who we are.

*Take chances, make mistakes. That's how you grow.
Pain nourishes your courage. You have to fail in order
to practice being brave. ~ Mary Tyler Moore*

All trials should not be viewed as a *hindrance* but may be perceived as a *helpful nudge* in the right direction. Disappointments do not have to produce calamity. Adopt an optimistic attitude. Always view your cup as half full, especially since God has the pitcher and is the One doing the pouring. God is pouring into you, quenching your thirst and needs; the brim of your cup is teeming with grace. As your cup runneth over, be ye filled and prepare to bless others from the overflow.

*Be the change that you wish to see in
the world. ~ Mahatma Gandhi*

When you remain steadfast about being ambitious, self-aware, and determined to manifest your dreams, regardless of the uphill battles, your drive becomes a powerful testimony of rumbustious faith. A display of grit can demonstrate to others how to handle turmoil. Every experience that a person may encounter, in some way, is universal. Someone, elsewhere, could be grappling with the same, exact struggle that you are currently battling. Please keep in mind that the rain falls on the just and the unjust, alike. God does not play favorites. Instead of moping and complaining, seek a positive solution to the problem. Incorporate strategies, devise a plan, and get into the proper formation to address any concerns.

We like to make a distinction between our private and public lives. But anyone trying to live a spiritual life will soon discover that the most personal is universal, the most hidden is the most public. ~ Henri J.M. Nouwen

Do not teeter-totter in excuses, but put forth a sincere effort toward resolve. *(Note: You can have your excuses or you can have success. You can't have both. ~ Jen Sincero)* Become determined to invest in approaches that are action-oriented to accomplish your goals. Create a proposal that is forward-driven. The past is just that... the past. It is helpful, but it is not the determining factor for your future. When you languish in what has happened, you forfeit your right to obtain and maintain imminent possibilities. Make the choice to look on the bright side of every situation.

We must all suffer one of two things: the pain of discipline or the pain of regret. ~ Jim Rohn

Live in a land of vision. Identify the "aha" moments that grasp your attention and need your efforts. What opportunities do you see that are ignored by others? How can you create something of substance and value? Every prodigious product or innovative solution that you bring forth, starts with an idea, a concept that you first conceive in your mind. *(Note: Everything is created twice, first in the mind and then in reality. ~ Robin S. Sharma)* Invest in your creativity. Visualize where you want to go in your life and keep your *"eyes on the prize."* If you are going to show up somewhere make sure that you actually *show up.* There is *power* in your *presence.*

Stand guard at the door of your mind. ~ Jim Rohn

When negativity tries to invade your space, do not succumb to it. Break any strongholds that attempt to corrupt your mind. Remember, what you constantly think about, eventually, you bring about. Do not fall prey to fear. When you succumb to fear, that means that you are afraid of something that hasn't even happened, yet. You are not certain how things will unfold, yet your mind forms an illusion of what could possibly occur and manipulate it into a devastating conclusion. When you think about it that way, it seems absurd to fear something that isn't even real. Do not *think* your fears into existence.

If my mind can conceive it, and my heart can
believe it- I can achieve it. ~ Muhammad Ali

Now, faith works the same way. You are hoping for something that isn't clearly evident; it hasn't happened yet. So, if you can negatively think your fears into reality, then you should utilize that same energy to *positively think* your hopes and dreams into existence. *Choose faith.* Put in the work and stay motivated. A positive life will never be the byproduct of negative cogitations. The more frequently and consistently that you block out the negative toxins, the more skilled you will become in recognizing and resisting them. You will gain a sense of self-control and an awareness that will make you more cognizant of your cognitive abilities.

People often say that motivation doesn't last. Well, neither
does bathing. That's why we recommend it daily. ~ Zig Ziglar

Maintaining a positive mindset is not only an attitude, it should become a way of life. *Positivity is a lifestyle.* The more positive you are in your daily actions, the more buoyant and determined you will be to continue moving towards your goals and creating the life that you desire. Your persistent contemplations will produce and attract these manifestations into your life. Your beliefs directly affect your behavior. Carefully, govern the meaning of your thoughts.

We cannot solve our problems with the same thinking
we used when we created them. ~ Albert Einstein

You have the capacity and willpower to enlarge your territory by broadening your mentality. The propensity to challenge yourself is to surround yourself with people that are already doing what you aspire to do. Nurturing the proclivity to succeed will never be realized by following an inert pattern and remaining satisfied with the status quo. Refuse to be a cautionary tale. Delve into another dimension of your character that will be completely unrecognizable to the people that know your past.

Change your thoughts and you change your
world. ~ Norman Vincent Peale

Proudly, exhibit your faith. You have self-discipline. Your mind is made up; whatever it takes, you will do it. You must stay hungry; you must constantly feed your dreams. Your blessing is built upon the hunger and thirst for what God has for you. Adhering to the call that is on your life is analogous to breathing; you *need to* do it. It is necessary; it is mandatory. The decision is made; you *must* fulfill your purpose.

I can't change the direction of the wind, but I can adjust
my sails to always reach my destination. ~ Jimmy Dean

You Have What It Takes

*Too many of us are not living our dreams because
we are living our fears. ~ Les Brown*

You absolutely have what it takes to reach your goals. Whatever you are passionate about, you can accomplish it. Sometimes, we must get out of our own way and navigate through the challenges because what we desire is on the other side of our oppositions. Raise your standards. Demand only the best from yourself. Develop a spirit of expectancy and anticipate great things to happen for you when you put forth a sincere effort.

*Nurture your mind with great thoughts, for you will never
go any higher than you think. ~ Benjamin Disraeli*

If you are not disciplined and diligent about forming the life that you want, then you may very well end up with a life that you did not strategically design. If you allow life to just happen to you, you will never maximize your full potential. You will never completely know what you are truly made of. Therefore, be mindful of every choice that you make and possess the confidence to handle any consequences that may materialize because of your decisions.

*Whatever the mind of {woman} can conceive
and believe, it can achieve. ~ Napoleon Hill*

God has bequeathed a gift within you. You should not let fears, insecurities, criticism, procrastination, doubt, or naysayers impede the journey towards your destiny. Do not let others deter your dreams. If they decided not to pursue their passion, that has nothing to do with you. Whatever they couldn't do should not interfere or influence your aspirations. You possess so much promise; you must not terminate your purposeful pursuits.

You must find a place in yourself where
nothing is impossible. ~ Deepak Chopra

Go after the very thing that you are afraid of and seize it. Allow your community to undergird you and to pray without ceasing that you will prevail. A win for you is a win for them. You are going to be just fine. You are significant. You are necessary. Your authentic life is about *becoming* and *being* the very best version of yourself. You need to give birth to your dreams. Your blessings are waiting for you.

Believe in yourself and all that you are. Know
that there is something inside you that is greater
than any obstacle. ~ Christian Larson

You must be intentional about your life. Be unapologetic about establishing authentic intentions to cultivate the type of life that you desire to bring to fruition. You must live your life on purpose. Prepare to manifest your dreams. Although it may not look like much and your circumstances may not reflect it right now, please do not despise small beginnings. Always remember, that the oak tree was already inside the acorn. There is so much promise within you.

If we did all the things we are capable of doing, we would
literally astound ourselves. ~ Thomas A. Edison

Be intentional about every decision and action that you partake in to achieve your goals. Each day is a fresh opportunity to get started. Someone is waiting for you to operate in your gift. The world needs what you have to offer.

You can start out with nothing, and out of
nothing, and out of no way, a way will be
made. ~ Dr. Michael Bernard Beckwith

If you do not utilize your potential, it will lose its value and become worthless. You need to activate your potential. Are you willing to use and share the gifts that God has assigned to you? How can you use your talents as acts of service? You must sharpen and harness your skills. You have what it takes to make a difference. Please do not become disillusioned. If you are rebellious, there will be a consequence. When you squander your opportunities, God will use someone else and reward their obedience with the blessings that were initially ordained for you.

Our potential is one thing. What we do with it
is quite another. ~ Dr. Angela Duckworth

You are your own best advocate. *Strive for the excellence that will eventually become your legacy.* Reject the premise to accept anything less than the same eminence and quality that you are willing to extend. Do not wait for someone else to extol you, validate you, or to grant you permission. You only need God's approval. Reflect on what's serving your highest purpose and rid yourself of the people or things that are running interference between you and your destiny.

Do not delay; pursue your possibilities. Someone is waiting and needing your story to model for them how you survived your encumbrances. Your example is going to help set them free from their bondage. You have a riveting testimony to share. Your *courage* may potentially *encourage* someone else to chase their dreams. *(Note: You are the answer to someone else's problem.)*

Be patient with yourself. Self-growth is tender, it's holy
ground. There's no greater investment. ~ Stephen Covey

You must believe in yourself. *Whatever You Can Dream.... You Can Do.* Never become so comfortable in your current situation that you become static. You must not cease to produce. If you do not continue to evolve, you will become extinct. Always strive for greatness in all that you do. Adopt a kingdom mindset of excellence, distinction, and *elevation.*

Don't let what you cannot do, interfere with
what you can do. ~ John Wooden

Disrupt your current mentality and recondition your thoughts in the areas that you deemed necessary. Embody the confidence that you need to walk in your destiny. *If you do not give up, you will win.* God wants to use **you**. *You have what it takes.* Begin today. *Start Now.*

Go confidently in the direction of your dreams. Live
the life you have imagined. ~ Henry David Thoreau

Take Action

---

*If you can't fly then run, if you can't run then walk, if you
can't walk then crawl, but whatever you do, you have to
keep moving forward. ~ Dr. Martin Luther King, Jr.*

It is extremely crucial that you set your intentions and put forth the actions to ensure that your plans are manifested. Be very deliberate about what you would like to accomplish and begin the process to get things done. Determine what ignites you. Now here is a little secret: *"Psst… if you do nothing, you will get nothing."* When you decide the steps that you will take and actually get started… you will reap tremendous results.

---

*The way to get started is to quit talking
and begin doing. ~ Walt Disney*

Hypothetically, let's assume that you have determined what your intent will be. You are very proud of this decision. But, you cannot purchase anything with intentions. Unused intentions are void and invalid. Some of our best intentions fail because we neglect to construct a strategic system of execution to reap our desired outcomes. You must vehemently commit to transitioning from inspiration to perspiration and get started. Put in the work… *now.*

Procrastination is not a good habit. ~ Bill Gates

In addition, to setting your intentions, you must ***do*** the work. It may take aspiration, hard work, perspiration, determination, loss of sleep, possibly shedding a few tears, and getting your hands dirty to achieve your goals. Let's review, primarily, believing in yourself, establishing your *why* and setting the intention lays the foundation; these are the first important steps. Next, you need to devise a plan to determine the best practices that should be implemented to bring your intentions into manifestation. Finally, you must initiate the process by putting the intentions into a motion that will amass into fruition. **Life Rewards Action.**

Action is the foundational key to all success. ~ Pablo Picasso

---

Life is too short and precious to decide to wait until you *"get it right."* Sometimes, you must learn or relearn as you go. We cannot take anything for granted; tomorrow is not promised to any of us. We only get one shot in this life. We all know too well that *time* is a precious commodity; it is fleeting, and it waits for no one. We only get one chance at this. This is not a dress rehearsal. Our life is center stage, whether we are ready for it or not: *Lights. Camera.* **Live.**

What we think or what we know or what we believe is, in the end, of little consequence. The only consequence is what we do. ~ John Ruskin

---

Referencing John 4:35-36, *The harvest is plenty, but the workers are few. You will reap what you sow.* Each one of us has an assigned task to fulfill. I can empathize that you may be tentative of taking risks. You would prefer not to face the possibility of rejection or failure. But, you cannot always play it safe. *(Note: The life that you may be living, may not be the life that God has in store for you. ~ Bishop T.D. Jakes)* Be courageous enough to face the fear. Your faith must dominate fear. Remember, that sometimes rejection could be a push to go in a different direction. You may need to reconstruct. Do not measure your value or self-worth based upon the world's acceptance or expectations. Do not be frightened to take the leap. When you jump, you will become airborne. *(Note: Sometimes your only available transportation is a leap of faith. ~ Margaret Shephard)* Your safety net will miraculously appear or you may even just begin to fly.

Start where you are. Use what you have.
Do what you can. ~ Arthur Ashe

Whatever dream that you possess, whatever goal that you yearn to achieve is possible. Everything is possible... *just go for it.* If you deny yourself the chance to see what you could really become, you may regret it. *(Note: The dreaming has to be backed up by the doing. ~ Carrie Wilkerson)* You cannot afford to be passive. That yearning and pull within you is there for a reason. You have nothing to lose. But, if you do not try... essentially, you may have everything to lose. Stop playing it safe; get out of your comfort zone. **Do. Something. Different.** Pray about your purpose and be prepared to act on the answers that you receive. *(Note: Daily, apply actions to your affirmations.)*

I have been impressed with the urgency of doing.
Knowing is not enough; we must apply. Being willing
is not enough; we must do. ~ Leonardo da Vinci

Trust your intuition and take the necessary steps to follow your instincts. Take small steps if you must because each mini-step will get you little closer than you were before. Do not give up; be relentless because all you need is one "yes" from God. *(Note: Commit to the Lord whatever you do, and He will establish your plans. ~ Proverbs 16:3)* Activate your full potential. Envision how you wish your life was designed at this very moment. Now, assess your life's current situation. *Are your vision and your reality one and the same?* If not, then you must take immediate action. Develop a sense of urgency and make it happen. Do not be afraid to jump; you may just soar like an eagle. *You were born to soar.* What are you waiting for? *Go. See.* **DO.**

Let today be the day, you love yourself enough to
no longer just dream of a better life. Let it be the
day, you act upon it. ~ Dr. Steve Maraboli

Fail Forward

Ever tried. Ever failed. No matter. Try Again.
Fail again. Fail better. ~ Samuel Beckett

If you were given the directive to choose one word that describes you, what would it be? *Intelligent, loving, compassionate, powerful, successful, mother, wife, CEO...* Or would you select the adjectives: failure, insecure, lonely, weak, damaged, or afraid? Your choice speaks volumes about how you perceive yourself. What you say about yourself matters more than what anyone else could ever say about you. Words are seeds. The very seeds that you plant, you will reap and they will manifest into your life. Therefore, please choose your words/seeds wisely.

Death and life are in the power of the tongue: and they
that love it shall eat the fruit thereof. ~ Proverbs 18:21

Do not become enticed or seduced by your title. The presence of God is more potent than any position. Consequentially, you should not confuse *what you do* with *who you are*; *doing* is very different from *being*. Analyze your thoughts and make the necessary reformations to any negative patterns. You can deduce that your words can evoke positive or negative emotions. *What* you think has everything to do with *who* and *where* you are. Do not permit self-perceived failures to hijack your vision. Allow your words to be a shield of strength that only speaks life into your circumstances. You must be self-motivated and optimistic about your life. Effectively utilize your words and language to propel you forward.

Come to the edge, He said. They said: We are afraid.
Come to the edge, He said. They came. He pushed
them, And they flew... ~ Guillaume Apollinaire

Do not become so fixated on the losses that you abandon all the achievements and wins that you have acquired. Likewise, do not place too much stock on what you have or have not accomplished, but instead on who you are... right now, in this very moment. Difficulties arise to rouse your ambition. Do you have the tenacity and energy to persevere despite any problems that you may have to combat? Do not become discouraged. Maintain your self-control. Stay above the fray. Please believe that for every door that is closed, it will eventually lead you to another door that *will* open.

Ninety-nine percent of all failures come from
people who have made a habit of making
excuses. ~ George Washington Carver

The vivid terms that you adopt to describe your experience, will manifest to become your reality. Your selection of vocabulary is likened to powerful, brandishing swords that can be either protective or damaging. Words can build up or tear down. Your diction can be manipulated into an empowerment source. Your words can change your attitude, your experiences and, ultimately, your entire life. Make a conscious choice to only select the vernacular that will encourage, hearten, inspire, and fortify you to be the biggest and very best version of yourself.

Do not judge me by my successes, judge me by how many
times I fell down and got back up again. ~ Nelson Mandela

What you say can completely shift your perspective. You must decipher which personal crises were beneficial, while also immediately releasing any traces of negativity. Failure formulates great road maps. Do not languish over mistakes. You must cogitate on the solutions. Reassessing your setbacks as well-calculated setups to embark upon a new path allows you to reconfigure your circumstances and, if plausible, to begin anew. There is only one direction that your life should be geared towards and that is forward.

There is no discovery without risk and what you risk reveals what you value. ~ Jeanette Winterson

To be successful, you must take methodical action and typically, this means taking risks. Consequently, you cannot afford to not take a risk. Be willing to bet on yourself. Put forth genuine efforts and not excuses, to live your best life. You, first and foremost, must believe in yourself. *You* are your own best investment.

For every failure, there's an alternative course of action. You just have to find it. When you come to a roadblock, take a detour. ~ Mary Kay Ash

Do not become comfortable with conformism. Nurture a mindset of being extraordinary. Surround yourself with exceptionally creative, driven, and intelligent visionaries. Apply your gifts, skills, and talents in a fashion that will assertively ignite such a spark of passion and resilience within you that you readily and courageously tackle any tasks, challenges, or obstacles that come your way. Your faith should always be bigger than fear. Make the choice to be faithful, not fearful to live the life you were meant to live. Having hope refuels your vigor to spark an irrepressible belief in your capability to succeed. Life is what you make of it and you must make profound choices that will demonstrate your ability to initiate compelling changes that will stimulate your personal growth.

If something is important enough, even if the odds are against you, you should still do it. ~ Elon Musk

It is never too late to make a positive transformation and become immersed in your search of discovering a life of purpose. You will gain a boost of self-confidence and exhibit an abundance of happiness when you maximize your potential doing what you love to do. You possess the power within to simply **be**. When you allow yourself to just **be**... you do not need an adjective to describe you. Your mere presence humbly exudes who you are. You recognize your value. You are amazing. You are magnificent. You are brilliant. You are persistent. You are a masterpiece. You are incredible. You are important. You are valuable. You are loved. You are the truth. *You are an Answer.*

Failure should be our teacher, not our undertaker.
Failure is delay, not defeat. It is a temporary
detour, not a dead end. ~ Denis Waitley

You are life's student. As long as life continuously teaches you, you will continue to learn. Do not become frustrated, agitated, or stressed out wanting a situation to be something that it isn't. When you do not become aligned with the supreme calling that is on your life, you will be redirected and it may take longer than intended to reach your destination. During the interim, proceed to live an interesting and full life.

Be brave enough to take chances; it's okay if you make some mistakes along the way. It is natural to feel terrified, but you must get out of your comfort zone and explore the edge of the cliff. Nothing extraordinary or revolutionary can be created from a space of comfortable confinement. *(Note: A person who never made a mistake never tried anything new. ~ Albert Einstein)* You do not become successful by staying on the ledge, being timid, nor by playing it safe or small.

Anyone who has achieved anything in life knows that
challenges and failures are necessary components of
success. Because those hard times are what shape you
into the person you're meant to be. ~ Michelle Obama

Even if a venture is not the success that you had hoped for, you will still gain pertinent insight. Failing does not make you a failure. By giving yourself permission to fail, you are giving yourself permission to fly. No one currently at your same level or beneath you should be able to tell you how high *you* can rise. Never let someone that didn't execute their dreams attempt to extinguish your dreams. *No matter what, keep trying.* Embrace your ups and downs, but most importantly live, learn, and enjoy the process.

Fall seven times, stand up eight. ~ Japanese Proverb

Never lose hope or faith, because every alternate path will *still* lead you to your destiny. So, therefore, your setbacks are just as significant and valuable as your victories. Your losses and wins are one and the same. You need to evoke your prior knowledge regarding what works for you and what doesn't work. The fiascos are a module of life's curriculum. If you consistently only *fail forward*, it's truly not a failure at all. *In actuality, you are simply evolving.*

Examples of Individuals Who Failed Forward:

*Most great people have attained their greatest success just
one step beyond their greatest failure. ~ Napoleon Hill*

- *Sara Blakely* revolutionized women's shapewear with Spanx, but in an industry run by mostly men, at the time, no one understood her billion-dollar idea. Fortunately, she did not give up.

- *Jack Canfield* co-founder and co-author of Chicken Soup for the Soul was rejected by many publishers - *144 publishers*. I am not certain how many authors would have continued to persevere after so many rejections or at the very least begun to have some self-doubt. His display of faith, tenacity, and resilience was absolutely incredible. The Chicken Soup for the Soul series has been groundbreaking.

- *Walt Disney* was told he wasn't creative enough. Yes, **the** Walt Disney that went on to create the most magical, happiest place on earth.

- *Henry Ford* went bankrupt multiple times but refused to compromise his vision for the perfect American-made vehicle. He went on to create the very successful Ford Motor Company that revolutionized automobiles and became a very, very wealthy man.

- *Bishop T.D. Jakes* has been lauded as America's Best Preacher by Time magazine. He has over 40 years in ministry, an executive producer, author, CEO, music label owner, songwriter, talk show host, humanitarian, advisor to presidents and dignitaries around the world. His wisdom, esteemed reputation, and influence reaches far and wide. But, before all of this astonishing, renown prominence, he dug ditches, received government assistance, utilities were cut off, and his vehicle was repossessed.

• *Steve Jobs* was fired from his own company... Apple *is* Steve Jobs. You cannot speak of one without mentioning the other.

• *Michael Jordan* was once cut from his high school basketball team because he was erroneously labeled as having a "lack of skill". If he had given up, he would have never fulfilled his purpose. And, ultimately, he wouldn't be recognized as arguably one of the greatest basketball players in NBA history.

• *Tyler Perry* took a risk and spent every cent that he had to invest into his dream, a stage play, and it was an epic failure. He kept trying but was still unsuccessful for several years. Although he became homeless, he refused to give up and gives all credit to his faith and God's grace. Now, he is a successful mogul, playwright, executive producer, director, screenwriter, author, songwriter, humanitarian, studio owner, employer, actor, creator of the larger-than-life persona Madea, *etc.* The Tyler Perry brand is a mega-successful conglomerate.

• *Steven Spielberg* was rejected from film school three times. If he would have given up, we wouldn't have been able to enjoy this visionary's successful movie masterpieces. For example, the productions of The Color Purple, ET, Schindler's List, Jurassic Park, Jaws, Saving Private Ryan, Catch Me If You Can, *etc.*

• *Oprah Winfrey,* **the** Oprah, the revered Ms. O, a mogul, legend, philanthropist, visionary, *O* Magazine founder, network founder and owner, author, the undisputed queen of daytime talk shows, actress, executive producer, *etc.*, and the best friend, mother, sister, aunt, role model, teacher, and inspiration to millions was raised in rural Mississippi by her grandmother at a time when even a small semblance of her current life would have been considered outlandish, far-fetched, inconceivable, not even remotely possible. She was also demoted/fired from a position in

Baltimore because she was deemed "unfit for TV" and I know, we all think, "that can't be right", but it happened. Yet, we must agree that, ultimately, it all worked out for her good.

I had to make a very conscious decision that I would rather flirt with failure than never dance with my joy. ~ Wes Moore

There are so many, many more individuals that we could add to the *Fail Forward List*. Here are just a few additional examples:

Mara Brock Akil, Jessica Alba, Muhammad Ali, Sophia Amoruso, Maya Angelou, Mary Kay Ash, Zain Asher, Lucille Ball, Tyra Banks, Jeff Bezos, Arthur Blank, Michael Bloomberg, Tom Brady, Richard Branson, Adam Braun, Scooter Braun, Rosalind Brewer, Les Brown, Warren Buffet, Ursula Burns, Gigi Butler, Joseph Campbell, Holley Carter, Truett Cathy, Claudia Chan, Kenneth Chenault, Julia Childs, Roy Choi, Winston Churchill, Ta-Nehisi Coates, Paulo Coelho, Kat Cole, Sean Combs, Misty Copeland, Mark Cuban, Viola Davis, Ellen DeGeneres, Leonardo DiCaprio, Jack Dorsey, Andrew Dreskin, Kevin Durant, Ava DuVernay, Marian Wright Edelman, Thomas Edison, Albert Einstein, Larry Ellison, Tim Ferris, Adam Fleischman, Harrison Ford, Marie Forleo, Devon Franklin, Chris Gardner, Tony Gaskins, Bill Gates, Berry Gordy, Earl G. Graves, Kevin Hart, Mellody Hobson, Lewis Howes, Ariana Huffington, Cathy Hughes, Samuel L. Jackson, LeBron James, Daymond John, Dwayne "The Rock" Johnson, Earvin "Magic" Johnson, John H. Johnson, Linda Johnson-Rice, Robert L. Johnson, Jon Bon Jovi, Tom Joyner, Gayle King, Martin Luther King, Jr., Stephen King, Mastin Kipp, Phil Knight, Debra Lee, John Lewis, Jamie Kern Lima, Abraham Lincoln, Heather Lindsey, George Lucas, Jack Ma, Julianne Malveaux, Nelson Mandela, Stephanie Meyer, Elon Musk, Diana Nyad, Hazel R. O'Leary, Will Packer, Thomas Paine, Michelle Phan, Kevin Plank, Sidney Poitier, Robert Redford, Shonda Rhimes, Condoleezza Rice, Tony Robbins, Robin Roberts, Sarah Jakes-Roberts, J.K. Rowling, Sheryl Sandberg, Colonel Sanders, Reshma Saujani, Howard Shultz, Jeff Skoll,

Will Smith, Bruce Springsteen, Sylvester Stallone, Bryan Stevenson, The Beatles, Billy Bob Thornton, Eckhart Tolle, Brian Tracy, Harriet Tubman, Tina Turner, Cicely Tyson, Iyanla Vanzant, Gary Vaynerchuk, Barbara Walters, Sam Walton, Vera Wang, Denzel Washington, Alli Webb, Serena Williams, Venus Williams, Robert W. Woodruff, Orville Wright, Wilbur Wright, Mark Zuckerberg, Gary Zukav, *etc.*

If ye abide in Me, and My words abide in you, ye shall ask
what ye will, and it shall be done unto you. ~ John 15:7

Although the evidence clearly stated something otherwise, they refused to give up. Their defiance to adhere to their current circumstances allowed them to successfully beat the odds. You must be so convinced of what God has promised you, that you stay focused, disciplined, and continue forging ahead. You will surely win if you do not give up.

History has demonstrated that the most notable winners
usually encountered heartbreaking obstacles before
they triumphed. They won because they refused to
become discouraged by their defeats. ~ B.C. Forbes

Freedom

---

*Freedom is not the absence of commitments, but
the ability to choose - and commit myself to
- what is best for me. ~ Paulo Coelho*

One of the human rights that most individuals desire is *freedom*. The freedom to make your own choices. The autonomy to make life-altering decisions: to love, to believe, to dream, to empower, to live, and to create a life that you truly aspire and deserve. You can initiate your pursuit of freedom with the vital step of releasing your past, which also requires rebuking every despairing memory that it entails. Although creating a clean slate may become a laborious and tedious task, it will be productive. The procedure will expunge any prolonged unresolved remnants and unburdened you. Your renewed freedom will assist with your overall efficiency.

---

*When you look at people who are successful, you will find
that they aren't the people who are motivated, but the ones
who have consistency in their motivation. ~ Arsène Wenger*

Have you ever felt sorry for yourself, a little longer than necessary? At times, obsessing over and wallowing in former circumstances may become addictive. Holding onto grief and turmoil lends itself to developing a victim mentality. You insentiently come to enjoy the self-made pity-parties. When you become accustomed to being bound, you forget what it feels like to be free. By neglecting to liberate your thoughts, unwittingly, you can often delay your own healing.

---

*Only you can take inner freedom away from yourself, or
give it to yourself. Nobody else can. ~ Michael A. Singer*

But when you fully let go of your past and come to peace with the closure of it, you become enlightened. The fallacies of never being able to move forward will come to a halt because that excuse is not valid. You can truly be *present*. You can fully enjoy the moment and the space of *Now*. Take a second to breathe in and absorb all that *was*, *is*, and *will be* in your life. Many strive to grasp the liberties that freedom affords us when we become empowered to freely and wholeheartedly pursue our dreams. Bravely navigate through an influx of options, risks, and opportunities to discern what you want out of this life. Being able to make a decision is the quintessential epitome of what freedom is. The freedom to *choose*.

> *Stand fast therefore in the liberty wherewith Christ*
> *has made us free, and be not entangled again*
> *with the yoke of bondage.* ~ *Galatians 5:1*

Mull over the following inquiries to assess your current situation:

- Are you putting forth the time and effort to maximize each day?
- Are you taking advantage of each opportunity that could possibly change the landscape and trajectory of your life?
- Are you carefully crafting out an agenda that allows you to strategically master your goals?
- Are you enthusiastically designing a path that leads you toward your destiny?
- How are you making your time count?

> *We must believe that we are gifted for something, and that*
> *this thing, at whatever cost, must be attained.* ~ *Marie Curie*

Do not waste your abilities living out someone else's visions. Attempting to duplicate someone's else life is a waste of the person that you truly are and the person that you were meant to be. You are blessed with the freewill to *be* and *do* whatever your heart desires. Set your intentions and meaningfully go about the business of manifesting your wildest dreams. Activate your ambitions and stay the course of being faithful to your mission. Mediocrity and excellence are counterproductive. Do not settle on traditionalism, being lackluster, or a lame run-of-the-mill. There is nothing average about you. You are free to be as original and creative as you please. Live as if each day of your life is a gift and a cause for celebration, because it absolutely is.

> *The best day of your life is the one on which you decide your life is your own. No apologies or excuses. No one to lean on, rely on, or blame. The gift is yours – it is an amazing journey – and you alone are responsible for the quality of it. This is the day your life really begins. ~ Bob Moawad*

Be protective of your dreams and desires. They are the gateway to your spirit and peace. Remain focused on engaging in activities, pleasantries, and opportunities that bring you enjoyment. You were created to be incomparable. Do not waive your rights to be vocal about your identity, expectations, and boundaries. When you are naïve or become preoccupied, the outcome can be detrimental to your clarity. Distractions limit your effectiveness. When you remain disciplined and focused, you are more adept to make better choices.

Take a moment to reflect:

- What kind of person do you yearn to become?
- What do you really desire to be manifested in your life?
- What contributions will you make to help improve society?

Whatever your responses are, please realize that you have the freedom to live out these declarations. *You are free to choose the direction of your life.* Intentional decisions and deliberate actions are the gems that will help you to create an authentic life. Ultimately, it is your choice.

> *The question isn't who is going to let me; it's who is going to stop me. ~ Ayn Rand*

Chapter IV: Being Empowered
Self-Coaching Session

1. Have you ever struggled with self-doubt? Please elaborate.

2. Have you forgiven yourself for past mistakes? List them. If not, when will you start the healing process?

3. How do you make yourself a priority? If you have not made yourself a priority, when will you start? Commit to a timeframe.

4. Have you given up on your dreams? Why or why not?

5. What are the dreams or goals that you have that are awaiting you to take action? When will you start? Commit to a deadline.

6. What are you passionate about? What would you do if you weren't afraid? What would you do if you had a blank check?

7. Take a moment to ponder about what you are currently doing now, your career, or relationships. If you had a choice *(barring your financial responsibilities)*, would you still have the desire to do it? Do you believe it's your calling?

8. Do you feel that you are *Living Your Purpose*? Are you *Living What You Love*? Is fear holding you back from seeking true self-fulfillment? Please explain.

9. What are some situations/things/people that you have had to or need to say goodbye to? What are you looking forward to saying goodbye to during this season of your life? Why? Provide a specific date.

10. What are your 1, 3, 5, 10 year goals or plans? Please be specific.

11. Create a *Plan of Action* snapshot that outlines the necessary steps toward exercising your freedom of choice to create the life that you desire.

12. Be intentional about utilizing your power to create the life that you want. Today, make the decision to pursue your purpose and passion. Create an *Empowerment Statement*. Meditate daily on your new personal mantra.

13. Always remember that you are exceptional. How will you begin to reclaim your power today? Please provide a thorough response.

Chapter IV: Being Empowered
Self-Reflection Notes

_____

_____

_____

_____

_____

_____

_____

_____

_____

_____

_____

_____

_____

_____

_____

CHAPTER V

Elevated BY
BEING AUTHENTIC

*To be nobody but yourself, in a world which is doing
its best, night and day, to make you everybody else,
means to fight the hardest battle any human can
fight, and never stop fighting. ~ e.e. cummings*

Be Unapologetically Authentic

*The privilege of a lifetime is to become
who you truly are. - C.G. Jung*

The most precious gift that you can give to others, and most importantly to yourself, is to be your *authentic self.* When you can embrace who you truly are, your self-acceptance will open numerous doors for you. Being audaciously empowered and unapologetically authentic furnishes you with the ability/skills to be truthful by accepting, loving, and honoring everything about yourself. This level of unambiguousness may inspire and empower someone else to do the same.

*Our self-respect tracks our choices. Every time
we act in harmony with our authentic self and
our heart, we earn our respect. It is that simple.
Every choice matters. ~ Dan Coppersmith*

Do not shroud yourself in oppressive distress hoping that you will not offend other individuals with your greatness, but instead, own your uniqueness in all its utmost glory. You were fearfully and wonderfully made in God's image. There is no denying your gifts and talents. You were created to embody and walk with *the ABCs:* authority, boldness, and confidence. There is so much power in your aura that it can literally change the atmosphere of any room that is graced with your presence. You are exceptional. A snippet of Marianne Williamson's poem, *Our Deepest Fear*, so vividly articulates this concept:

*Our deepest fear is not that we are inadequate. Our
deepest fear is that we are powerful beyond measure.
It is our light, not our darkness that most frightens us.
We ask ourselves, Who am I to be brilliant, gorgeous,
talented, fabulous? Actually, who are you not to be?*

When you become a servant, and give freely of your time without placing contingencies upon your contributions, you are destined to receive more in return for your efforts. You are heavily self-invested and own equity in your well-being. You are directly impacted by the outcomes *(positive or negative)* that may result in your life. There is too much at stake. Since you are really the only one with something to lose, wouldn't it be only fitting that you do what makes *you* happy? After all, it is *your* life. There are no pretenses or obligations to uphold. You can fearlessly *be* who you were meant to be. When you are endowed with grace and living life on your own terms, you purposefully encourage others to stand in their own truth.

The first and best victory is to conquer self. ~ Plato

When we give, we take the focus from ourselves and place it onto others. It's not about how much you can get paid, but more so, it's about how many people can you serve and inspire. *(Note: There is an apparent distinction between freely giving and being taken advantage of.)* We are afforded a freedom that allows us to strive to be a positive force and make a difference in someone else's life. We are all a work-in-progress and we can learn from each other daily.

I am unapologetically black and unapologetically
a woman. ~ Mellody Hobson

When you look within, you will realize that you have what it takes to perform at your maximum level. What God has placed inside of you will be manifested. Be the phenomenal woman basking in the glory of what all this delightfulness entails. When there are no falsities about your character, your true identity is authenticated. Your spirit is pure. Your mind, body, and soul are at peace. In bold genuineness, you can represent yourself candidly and confidently. The road to authenticity is a brave and noble path that is fulfilling and rewarding.

Authenticity requires a certain measure of vulnerability,
transparency, and integrity. ~ Janet Louise Stephenson

Upon releasing tempting and unproductive tendencies, you magnetize positive energy. When you tap into your authentic intentions, and genuinely *be* the person you were created to be, you will model to others that they do not have to live with constraints. You are posed to emulate God's plan for your life. Your life is your own and tomorrow is not promised to anyone. Cherish every moment by being exactly who you were meant to be. Trust your journey. Enjoy your transition. Live your truth.

We can't become what we need to be... by
remaining what we are. ~ Oprah Winfrey

Embrace and revel in your potential and the gifts that you are blessed with, and in the interim, you may enthuse someone else to muster the courage to live their best life, as well. Develop an astute sense of who you want to be and what you want out of life. Live in the enthralling and encompassing space of truth. *It is never too late to be unapologetically authentic.*

Enlightenment is the key to everything, and it
is the key to intimacy, because it is the goal of
true authenticity. ~ Marianne Williamson

What Are You Passionate About?

*Follow your passion, be prepared to work hard
and sacrifice, and, above all, don't let anyone
limit your dreams. ~ Donovan Bailey*

Occasionally, you may have been exposed to or pondered the question, *"What are you passionate about?"* when attempting to determine what you would like to do with your life. There is a preconceived notion that you must follow your passion; that discovering your passion will help to position you to discover your purpose. Is this true? Does passion necessarily equate to discovering your purpose? What is your belief? What speaks to you? What excites you? Many of us strive to make a profit from our passion. We'd all like to get paid for doing something that we would do for free because we love it so much.

*Choose a job that you love and you will never
work a day in your life. ~ Confucius*

Your passion is extremely powerful. It is *the* thing that you can effortlessly command. It is the channel that directs you to explore your inner inhibitions. It also redirects you when you feel an empty void. You intuitively realize that something is *out-of-sync*. It stimulates your curiosity and makes you yearn for *"something more."* People have left jobs, changed careers, ventured into entrepreneurship, relocated, taken risks, ended or forged new relationships all *because of* or the *lack of* passion.

*The biggest mistake people make in life is not trying to make
a living at doing what they most enjoy. ~ Malcolm S. Forbes*

Your passion will prompt you to become a life-long learner. At times, you may even forget to eat; passion becomes your fuel and nourishment. You will consistently study, experiment, explore, get up early or go to bed late… because you become so engulfed in the moment, that you lose track of time, doing what you feel passionate about. Doing what you feel compelled or driven to do.

You have to be burning with an idea, or a problem, or
a wrong that you want to right. If you're not passionate
enough from the start, you'll never stick it out. ~ Steve Jobs

Passion helps you to develop into the person that you truly desire to become. You walk with a purpose. People will recognize that you are a person that is going somewhere. You're on a mission; you have an assignment to fulfill. Passionate people transcends all expectations and project an authoritative demeanor. They are charismatic. Their back is straight, shoulders are squared displaying good posture; they stand tall. Their head is held high. Their handshake is firm, while making direct eye contact. They appear powerful, distinguished, and possess a winner's mentality. Their confidence is evident and their presence commands respect. They emit high-frequency levels of energy. Their enthusiasm is contagious.

Nothing is as important as passion. No matter what you
want to do with your life, be passionate. ~ Jon Bon Jovi

But, passion can also be very complex. There are layers within your passion. Your passion possesses its own layers of passions. When you discover one area that you find interesting, it may lead you along another avenue that can guide you to scope out other enjoyable adventures. Have you ever noticed how people 're-invent' themselves and are just as, if not even more than, successful as before? They are tapping into their passion's passions. It becomes a spin-off that will create platforms and exposure. You do not have to neglect anything; it just shows how versatile and multifaceted you are. *(Note: It is possible to have more than one purpose and it's possible to have more than one passion.)* You are ambitious, creative, and multitalented. You can continuously evolve and rebrand yourself. When you are passionate about your purpose, you are effortlessly driven to exploration. You seek out and create resolutions.

My mission in life is not merely to survive, but to thrive;
and to do so with some passion, some compassion,
some humor, and some style. ~ Dr. Maya Angelou

Embodying your passion exhibits the appeal of being spontaneous; you are a risk taker. You find pleasure in successfully defying the odds. You feel empowered when you are validated for trusting your intuition. It encourages you to continue to be stirred, creative, and exhibit self-expression. You are primed to not only reside, but to prosper in the beautiful spaces of self-awareness and enlightenment.

Forget about the fast lane. If you really want to fly, just
harness your power to your passion. ~ Oprah Winfrey

Your poise and grandeur are on full display. Having passion is admirable and vitally important, *but the pinnacle is to have a vision.* You must know what you are going to do with this passion. *(Note: The only thing worse than being blind is having sight but no vision. ~ Helen Keller)* How will it be incubated, implemented, and function in your life?

Passion is one great force that unleashes creativity,
because if you're passionate about something, then
you're more willing to take risks. ~ Yo-Yo Ma

Align what you are passionate about with providing a much-needed service that can have a positive impact on society. *(Note: Doing what you love is the cornerstone of having abundance in your life. ~ Wayne Dyer)* Possessing the freewill to investigate, study, and serve in an area that splendidly interests and excites you is truly a blessing. Passion galvanizes you to maximize your efforts. Commitment to grinding and hustling at your highest peak produces a stellar performance that establishes a rhythmic pace in your life that generates a healthy and balanced flow. You become *in-sync* with the universe. It promotes an effervescent happiness, a healthy well-being, and tremendous enrichment. For many, the power of passion is parallel to breathing. When you tap into your passion and purpose, you will become fully immersed in truly *LIVING What You LOVE...*

There is no passion to be found playing small,
in settling for a life that is less than the one you
are capable of living. ~ Nelson Mandela

Happiness Is a Choice

Never authorize someone the power to determine
what makes YOU happy. ~ Dr. Keke

Self-love and self-acceptance are prominent necessities that you should epitomize as prerequisites for indulging in happiness. Be grateful and embrace everything *(the good, bad, and ugly)* about yourself and *'love the skin that you are in.'* Each crack, splinter, or fragment wholly forms the texture that makes you unique. When you discard the idea of having to achieve perfection but instead choose to accept your beautiful imperfections, you grant yourself the permission to love yourself and thrive in the space of acceptance, naturalness, and candor. Always remember that you are God's spectacular creation. The *same God* that created mountains, oceans, the entire universe… *created and lives within you*. Each part of you is purposefully and beautifully designed.

Everything has beauty, but not everyone can see. ~ Confucius

You should not evoke an unrealistic image or succumb to unnecessary self-induced pressures. Your blemishes give you a special attractiveness and compliment your diversity. Your flaws make you fabulous because they make you human, eccentric, and real. And when you are real, you are relatable. Don't believe that *when* you have a *perfect* life, you will *then* become happy. A positive life situation isn't the cause of happiness. It is the yielded result. Happiness comes from acknowledging that you are more than enough…. *just as you are.*

The answer lies within ourselves. If we can't
find peace and happiness there, it's not going to
come from the outside. ~ Tenzin Palmo

Typically, by nature, women are nurturers. We tend to want to 'fix' everything involving people and situations. Being helpful is a wonderful characteristic to embody, but being a *shero* can be physically, mentally, emotionally, and even financially depleting. It is exhausting. Especially, if you neglect your own needs. Take the superwoman cape off and cancel the show. Or better yet, keep the cape on and for once, be your own *shero* and rescue yourself.

> *When one door of happiness closes, another opens, but often we look so long at the closed door that we do not see the one that has been opened for us.* ~ Helen Keller

Mandate that you make yourself a priority in your own life. There must be a balance. It is vital that you do not become so negligent of your own needs that you forget to include yourself on your daily *To-Do* list. (*Note: I'm working my happiness like a full-time job.* ~ Gabby Bernstein) When you take the appropriate time to reassemble, rejuvenate, nurture, and invest in yourself, you are more likely to be a blessing to others. When you are truly happy, you genuinely want to be a blessing to someone else.

> *How wonderful it is that nobody need wait a single moment before starting to improve the world.* ~ Anne Frank

When you recognize that you own the power of making yourself happy, it can be very redeeming. *You* should be one of the best, most interesting people that you know. If someone or something is an impediment to your joy, you can choose to disassociate from the situation. You have the right to take care of you. Nothing or no one should possess the power to make you feel less than. Take responsibility for creating your own happiness.

No one can make you feel inferior without
your consent. ~ Eleanor Roosevelt

Doing what makes you happy is a daring move. It takes courage to conceive a vision and initiate a plan of action to pursue your dreams. At times, your decisions may not garner any applause, but you must remain true to yourself. Explore to determine what you are passionate about and go for it. No progress can be made by being timorous on the sidelines. You must get in the game and become a part of the action.

Align your vision with your purpose and the process will flow effortlessly. Gain a fresh way of thinking and you will acquire a renewed outlook on life. Changing your perspective may lead to discovering your true calling and power. What you begin to manifest inwardly will materialize outwardly. *Happiness is a choice.* And when you chose to be happy, you chose *You*!

I have decided to be happy, because it's
good for my health. ~ Voltaire

Who Am I?

> *The only person you are destined to become is the*
> *person you decide to be. ~ Ralph Waldo Emerson*

I persistently pondered the inquiry, *"Who Am I?"* I constantly prayed and meditated about this profound question. I yearned to uncover God's purpose and perfect plan for my life. I needed to reveal my true character. I knew my genetic makeup; my parents were responsible for that. I needed to discover my characteristics and emotional makeup. This is my responsibility. I began to truly fast, pray, and to seek guidance. I asked the Lord to help me to define my persona. I knew my current state of being, but I needed to assess where I came from, in order, to gain a deeper comprehension and connection for where I was headed. I needed to go within myself, to find myself.

> *When I let go of what I am, I become*
> *what I might be. ~ Lao Tzu*

Wouldn't it be tragic to live your whole life and not know your true character, your true identity, your destiny, or God's purpose for your life's journey? In Genesis 32:24-30, God asked Jacob what was his name. Now surely, Jacob should have known his own name. It was the only name he has had his entire life. But, suddenly it is now being called into question. There was an influx of uncertainty. What does this mean? Could he have been living a lie; operating or performing under pretense?

The name Jacob means trickster, con artist. His family lineage was comprised of liars, conniving and manipulative people. He was one of them. But, when Jacob wrestled with God and declared that despite his past mistakes and negative experiences, *"I will not let You go until You bless me."* Not only did God bless him... He renamed him. *Jacob became Israel.* Jacob had lived his whole life as one person, but now he has experienced an awakening. He is now transformed. His whole identity was being changed. It changed for the better. Although he still looked the same on the outside, he was no longer the same on the inside.

Now, if someone were to ask you or me what were our names, it would be silly for us to hesitate to answer. But what if we continued to believe and live as though we were a 'Jacob', when God has already predestined us to be '*Israel*'? It is so important that once you have been reborn, renewed (renamed), and reestablished that you do not revert to whom or what you used to be or do. Allow your inner transformation to manifest itself and be reflected externally.

What we achieve inwardly will change outer reality. ~ Plutarch

When you discover your purpose, you are no longer the same as you were before. Is this what it means to be born again? We need to put '*new wine into new wineskins.*' When we are in the hands of the Potter, He will shape us with love and grace when we cry out and glorify Him. God doesn't care about the cracks in our foundation. He will address and correct all the blemishes if we invite Him to do so. At any time, you can welcome the Lord into your heart. When the Lord breathes new life into you, you are roused and recommenced. Isn't that remarkable? Pray that He removes anything that is not like Him out of you and your life.

I am not what I ought to be, I am not what I want to be, I am not what I hope to be in another world; but still I am not what I once used to be, and by the grace of God I am what I am. ~ John Newton

If you are not exactly where you want to be, still thank God that you are not where you used to be. God can and will break any generational curses and restore you. Regardless of our unsavory past, God will use the least of them. Many are called, but few are chosen. He will call and use the most unlikely and the unqualified. Don't feel less than; you belong in the room. The Lord endorses you. You deserve a seat at the table. *(Note: If they don't give you a seat at the table, bring a folding chair. ~ Shirley Chisholm)* Reference prominent figures in the Bible that had sordid histories that God still used in a mighty way as His surrogates: *Moses, Paul, David, Peter, Rahab, etc.* He will do the same for you. He will do the same for me.

Therefore, if anyone is in Christ, he {she} is a new creation; old things have passed away; behold, all things have become new. ~ 2 Corinthians 5:17

From this day forward, be intentional about every decision that you make. God has embedded freewill within each of us. You can always reinvent yourself. You can start at any moment that you choose to; it is up to you. The past has happened and there is nothing you can do to change it, but you can utilize that wisdom to help shape and mold your future.

Sometime I think; and sometime I am. ~ Paul Valéry

Do not dim your light to pacify others' insecurities. Do not try to hide or downplay your confidence and strength. For it is within your light that the Lord is amplified and glorified in the presence of others. Let me advise you of something that is extremely important, "knowing who you are **not**… is just as critical as knowing who you *are*…"

At the center of your being, you have the answer; you know who you are and you know what you want. ~ Lao Tzu

---

I believe that life follows a systematic format. Naturally, it may vary by individuals, on a case-by-case basis. Based upon our chronological age, the *Life Philosophy Flow* may be categorized as:

Life Philosophy Flow:

20s- exploration, finding yourself, coming into your own

30s- desiring and yearning for knowledge, growth, self-awareness, identifying and correcting any mistakes that you may have made in your 20s

40s- obtaining stability, a sense of direction, seeking fulfillment, embracing confidence

50s & older – feeling a sense of completeness/wholeness, in your element, wiser, loving life and the skin that you are in, creating your legacy, being unapologetically authentic

---

Close your eyes and imagine the best version of you possible. That's who you really are. Let go of any part of you that doesn't believe it. ~ C. Assaad

---

Some individuals do mature faster, while others seem to remain childish. Sometimes, you can feel trapped at the same age for years. Others may have grown up too fast and via a mid-life crisis, retroactively revert in time attempting to recapture their lost youth. There are always exceptions to the rule. Regardless of where you are on the continuum, hopefully, you will be able to sincerely gauge an honest comprehension of your God-assigned identity and sense of purpose.

Many people die with their music still in them. Why is this so? Too often it is because they are always getting ready to live. Before they know it, time runs out. ~ Oliver Wendell Holmes

---

Be true to yourself. Your potential and possibilities are limitless. It's never too late to start living your dreams. Start today; you'll be so glad that you did. One of my favorite scriptures is Exodus 3:14, **"I AM THAT I AM."** Whenever we are in need, *God will become whatever we need Him to be.* Now when I mull over the question, *"Who Am I?"* I can confidently answer, *"I Am..."*

*I am not my thoughts, emotions, sense perceptions,
and experiences. I am not the content of my life. I am
Life. I am the space in which all things happen. I am
consciousness. I am the Now... I Am... ~ Eckhart Tolle*

Becoming the Woman, You Were Meant to BE...

> *Don't compromise yourself. You are all you've got. There is no yesterday, no tomorrow, it's all the same day. ~ Janis Joplin*

Have you ever struggled with feelings of insecurity or uncertainty? Unconsciously, have you ever compared yourself to other women? Has doubt ever entered your mind and a negative voice whispered that you don't measure up? Has it ever deceivingly chimed that *you're not good enough or worthy?* Well, you are not alone. Many other women have felt the exact same way. Do not buy into the fallacy that you are not good enough. You are a part of the collective.

Believe it or not, some other woman may be looking at you and feel that she doesn't measure or stack up against your beauty or credentials. As ironic as it may seem, women instinctively recognize talents and potential in other women. Failing to realize that she may possess those similar fortes and potential within herself. So often, the treasured gifts are neglected or are not even acknowledged by its owner.

> *Sometimes, I feel discriminated against, but it does not make me angry. It merely astonishes me. How can any deny themselves the pleasure of my company? It's beyond me. ~ Zora Neale Hurston*

You should never feel inadequate because of someone else's accomplishments. You are distinctively and exclusively designed to run your own race at your own pace. The self-acceptance of this knowledge is what makes every woman powerful, beautiful, special, and accomplished in her own right. Do not view other women as your *competition*, but instead as potential *collaborative partners*. *(Note: A flower does not think of competing with the flower next to it. It just blooms. ~ Zen Shin)* There is so much more to be gained when you collaborate instead of competing with one another. I promise you that there is enough success for everyone.

Delight yourself in the Lord and He will give
you the desires of your heart. ~ Psalm 37:4

It is so important not to focus on another woman's present glory, especially when you don't know what happens behind-the-scenes. You can't see the complete picture. The highlight reels are what's shown, but the rebirthing and transformation process can be extremely tramuatic. You can't see *one scene* of someone's life and think you know their *whole story.* Many achievements come at a high price. When you covet someone else's gifts and blessings, you never truly master your own promises, skills, and talents. You shortchange yourself, as well as, others.

You cannot eat potential. Potential is not tangible. You must bring forth the gifts that you possess within you, so that they may be manifested into something that is palpable, powerful, and beneficial. *What do you have to offer? How can you leave your positive imprint on the world?* Be candid... *When you look at yourself in the mirror, what do you see?* If you have not discovered your purpose, lean not unto your own understanding. With genuineness and humility, submit your petitions to the Lord, seek His guidance and direction, and get very still to receive your answer. If necessary, sequester yourself. *(Note: The quieter you become, the more you can hear. ~ Ram Dass)* Solitude can give you a fresh discernment. Muffle the outside voices and noise; become centered and be willing to listen with an open heart.

Learning is a gift. Even when pain is
your teacher. ~ Maya Watson

Do not shy away from your history. It is your story. Embrace your experiences. The past does not own you. If you choose to shrink instead of blossoming, you will deny yourself the opportunity to gracefully develop into the woman that you were meant to be. *(Note: It is never too late to be what you might have been. ~ George Eliot)* A part of your journey consists of developing and strengthening your astuteness, piquing your interests, skillfully shaping your resilience, toughening your outer layers of skin while softening your heart and features.

Your past experiences make you wiser and shine brighter because you have been through some "stuff" and you have learned a few things. Your wounds and scars are the symbols that provide evidence of your strength. The lessons were invaluable because they assisted in the seminal process of making you stronger, remarkable, humble, and virtuous. *(Note: A wise woman wishes to be no one's enemy; a wise woman refuses to be anyone's victim. ~ Dr. Maya Angelou)* Never forget that, *you are a woman of purpose. You are grace personified.*

> *Instead of looking at the past, I put myself ahead*
> *twenty years and try to look at what I need to do*
> *now in order to get there then. ~ Diana Ross*

Strategically take time out of the year, month, week and/or day to reflect on how much you have grown and matured. How the things that used to upset you and kept you up at night has lost its power and no longer has an effect on you. Now, you can sleep through that nonsense.

> *Strength and honor are her clothing; and she shall*
> *rejoice in time to come. ~ Proverbs 31:25*

Evaluate the depths of your maturity. Strip yourself of unnecessary titles, people, and tangible objects. When your mind is less cloudy and free of the clutter and outside influences, analyze who you are as a self-sufficient woman. Finding a *sense of self* will empower you to do and accomplish anything that you set your mind to do. There are no limits. Acknowledge that if it weren't for the grace that kept you, you don't know where you would be. The Lord created within you a clean heart and a fresh start.

Always be a first-rate version of yourself, instead of a second-rate version of somebody else.
~ Judy Garland

Therefore, you should never attempt to be a simple replica or duplicate someone else. *(Note: No one is you and that is your power. ~ Dave Grohl)* Your anointing and your favor are appointed specifically for you. Be so on top of your game, that you exude confidence. *You are Her...* and *She is You...*Take a moment to contemplate how *powerful* and *blessed* you truly are. *(Note: You have the ability to create life; there is absolutely nothing that you cannot achieve.)* You already have everything that you need *within* you. Tap into your potential, possibilities, promise, and power. ***YOU*** *are everything that you seek...*

You make me proud to spell my name,
W-O-M-A-N. ~ Dr. Maya Angelou

Stand in Your Truth

---

*The most courageous act is still to think
for yourself. Aloud. ~ Coco Chanel*

Live out loud and inspire others to do the same... When you unlock the door to your story, your truth may potentially free someone else. Most often life's most expensive lessons are learned during the most unexpected and inopportune times. Rest in the Lord. Value the simple things that life has to offer. We must condition ourselves to slow down, stand still and pay attention to the slightest minuscule element. We need to recognize the importance of small moments. There should be an acquired reverence for these intimate particulars.

---

*Everything will line up perfectly when knowing
and living the truth becomes more important
than looking good. ~ Alan Cohen*

When you discover the true importance of being patient, kind, and of service to others, it can unequivocally enhance your entire life. When you are comfortable enough to fully accept yourself, *failings and all*, you can be unapologetically authentic. Others can see the glitz and glamor that you have acquired now, but so few really know the hell that you may have went through to obtain and maintain your current eminence. A lot of people may want what you have, but they do not want to go through what you had to go through to get it.

Your candor about the complex difficulties that almost overtook you and divulging how you refused to give up on yourself can be a life-changing testament used to enlighten others. When you courageously *embrace* and *live* your truth, your confidence may be just the brave inspiration that someone needs to encourage them to unashamedly share their story.

I could not, at any age, be content to take my place by the
fireside and simply look on. Life was meant to be lived.
Curiosity must be kept alive. One must never, for whatever
reason, turn his back on life. ~ Eleanor Roosevelt

Many of us meticulously plan our itineraries in advance by the days, weeks, months, quarters or years. We carefully craft out the goals that we would like to accomplish. Make the decision to disrupt this pattern. Expose yourself to diverse challenges and spontaneously embark upon exotic adventures. Attempt to infuse something new and daring into your daily rituals to break up the monotony. Incorporate into your schedule the valor to seek activities that will incite joy and excitement. Participate in pursuits that stimulates your interests, enriches your creative expression, inspires you to laugh, to live fully and love more deeply.

I wish I could show you... the astonishing
light of your own being. ~ Hafez

When you begin to think and do things differently, you can expect different results. You are revolutionary and unapologetically amazing. When you live your life to the fullest and stand in your truth, not only does it motivate others to live their best lives; it will make your life richer and fuller as well. Because you are innovative, you weren't meant to be a carbon copy of someone else. You were meant to be your true self, without the fear of repercussions. You are courageous, tenacious, captivating, awesome, and vivacious. When you stand in your truth, simultaneously, *you are standing in your power.*

The woman who doesn't need validation from anyone is the
most feared individual on the planet. ~ Mohadesa Najumi

5 Tips to Cultivate an Intentional Life

The two most important days in your life are, the day you are born and the day you find out why. ~ Mark Twain

---

It is not by coincidence that you are here. You were born into this world for a precise reason. To discover what you were specifically created to do is one of the most exhilarating joys that you could ever experience. Being able to fulfill your purpose, as well as, add quality and substance to society is an ultimate satisfaction that exceeds beyond measure.

Unfortunately, sometimes when you comply with your need to be authentic, it may come with its own share of difficulties. Affording yourself the malleability to be shaped lends itself to your fluidity. Being willing to face these complications and persevere, equips you with the spirit and strength to tackle any deterrents. With hard work, consistency, focus, discipline, tenacity, and determination, you can create the intentional life that you desire and thrive.

If you are to live meaningfully, your life must have purpose and significance. Create an intentional life that adds quality, substance, and honors your authentic calling. ~ Dr. Keke

---

Strategies to Cultivate an Intentional, Authentic Life

I never dreamt of success. I worked for it. ~ Estee Lauder

---

1. **Recognize that Happiness Is Vital–** When you embody genuine happiness, you attract a level of success into your life. Focus on your priorities; maximize the moments that truly matter. Being

happy exemplifies the concept that you are appreciative of what you already possess. Being grateful for what you have right now, creates an opportunity for you to magnetize and receive more of what you need and want into your life.

We tend to forget that happiness doesn't come as a result of getting something we don't have, but rather of recognizing and appreciating what we do have. ~ Frederick Koenig

Furthermore, a level of happiness can also be generated when you are of great service to others. You will radiate bliss and invite more joy into your space. Remember happiness is not something that you can get from other people nor is it about collecting tangible items. Happiness is about *being* and *living* the best version of *your authentic self.*

2. **Establish a Supportive Community**– Your team should be comprised of people that are positive, supportive, and enthusiastic about your success. Their energy motivates you to excel to the highest version of your best self. And in return, you reciprocate the same gentility to them. They are your tribe. They are an extension of you. They understand you; *they just get you* and the feeling is mutual. When you are in the company of your village, their presence should make you strive higher. They are not envious or manipulative. They are not after what you have. They do not attempt to discourage your dreams. They are engaging, encouraging and accepting, yet candid with you.

Everyone may not understand or support your calling. Therefore, it is essential that you surround yourself with 'like-minded', remarkable people. There is power in proximity. Never let another individual tell you who you are. Cease giving others the authorization to define your identity or self-worth. Do not grant anyone the power to tell you what you can or cannot do nor permit them the privilege to tarnish your dreams. Stay true to your vision. *Be humble, yet, know your value.*

Be strong, be fearless, be beautiful. And believe that anything is possible when you have the right people there to support you. ~ Misty Copeland

---

Take an honest inventory of your relationships and ascertain if you have a positive community supporting you as you pursue your purpose. Make any audits that you warrant to be necessary. Assure that these individuals are in your life to support you intrinsically, and not solely to reap the benefits of your success. They are your cheerleaders and in return, you are theirs.

3. **Embrace the Power of "No"**- The word, *No*, can be deemed as a complete sentence. ~N.O.~ How you choose to spend your time defines who you are as a person. You must create a healthy balance in your life. Establishing boundaries are necessary to ensure that you do not become burned out or overwhelmed. Do not overcommit yourself only to later regret it. A choice should be made to reveal if you rather have popularity by appeasing everyone or would you prefer to obtain respect and peace. Your first obligation should be to yourself. Prioritize your agenda and ensure that you include yourself on it.

The difference between successful people and very successful people is that very successful people say "No" to almost everything. ~ Warren Buffet

---

No, can also mean saying *No*: to fear, low self-esteem, peer pressure, negativity, etc. You may have conquered some of life's toughest trials and now you refused to continue to be a victim, but instead, thrive as a victor. Your *"Nos"* make your *"Yeses"* more valuable. *Embracing the Power of No* is a strength and all about self-perception.

4. **Say "Yes" to New Opportunities**– Saying *Yes* to an array of opportunities and adventures exposes you to a whole, new world that you may have never known existed. New ventures await you if you are open to receiving them. Give yourself permission to discover what brings you joy, excitement, and motivation. *Yes,* can take you out of your comfort zone and make you vulnerable. Vulnerability exposes you to distinct layers of yourself. Taking risks can stretch you and make you grow in every area of your life. This firsthand exposure can usher you into an innovative world of possibilities.

If you're offered a seat on a rocket ship, don't ask what seat! Just get on. ~ Sheryl Sandberg

---

You will never know what you are truly capable of until you take a leap of faith. Some of life's best adventures result from taking the risk to jump. There may be some cuts and bruises along the way, but those bumps and lumps will heal. You have to bob and weave when your life circumstances change. Do not become sidelined by fear. Your leap of faith has the potential to become a launching pad. You will be amazed at how the safety net will instantaneously appear or the parachute will open just in the nick of time.

Surrender to what is. Say "yes" to life and see how life suddenly starts working for you, rather than against you. ~ Eckhart Tolle

---

The rewards of taking risks will always be more fulfilling than having regrets. Your willingness to be open and explore can even lead to developing new relationships. The wind beneath your wings will support you as you *fly, fly, fly*. Your **Yes** journey can place you on a path to self-discovery and self-reinvention.

5. **Make Informed-Decisions**– Cultivate a new mindset. One decision can absolutely change your entire life. Live boldly; be courageous. Discover the possibilities that await you. Be unapologetic about being brave, confident, and loving your true self. Do not become distracted by skepticism. Foster a space in your life that is designated solely for you and discovering your purpose.

Insanity is defined as doing the same thing over, and over, and over again, yet somehow expecting different results. Indecisiveness can be just as destructive. You need to make the decision to be dauntless about forging a path to your destiny. Change your thoughts. Visualize your future. Embrace faith. Be spontaneous and relentless. Stand in your truth. Act, speak, think, love, live, and lead differently. Be willing to change, grow, and evolve.

I am not a product of my circumstances. I am a product of my decisions. ~ Stephen Covey

Become enriched by exposure. Maximize your potential. Seize opportunities. Know your worth. Love yourself. Respect, honor, value, and trust yourself. Forgive yourself. Free yourself. Encourage yourself. Edify yourself. Empower yourself. Validate yourself. Bet on yourself. Reward yourself. Laugh at yourself. Reimagine yourself. Be true to yourself. Be more/full of yourself.

*The most difficult thing is the decision to act, the
rest is merely tenacity. ~ Amelia Earhart*

Live your life in such a way that at the end of each day, you are completely full. You can acknowledge that you did your very best. You performed at your optimum peak. Life isn't always about the destination; it is life's journey that provides you with the most colorful experiences, textures, and memories. To demonstrate authenticity, you must pursue your true purpose, be decisive, and become intentional about creating the life that you were destined to live. *Live your life on your terms. Be unapologetically authentic.*

*If there's a book that you want to read, but it hasn't been
written yet, then you must write it. ~ Toni Morrison*

As the author of your truth, assess how you would desire for your life's story to be read. If a new chapter is not properly developing in accordance to your outline, do not become exasperated nor should you succumb to writer's block. Do not stress about having to start over. Never give up. Seek various avenues of inspiration. Select new stimulating surroundings. Change your narrative. It is your prerogative if you need to insert *"To Be Continued..."*

*Failure is probably the most important factor
in all of my work. Writing is failure. Over and
over and over again. ~ Ta-Nehisi Coates*

Nothing materializes by happenstance. If the best part of your history hasn't been written, you must pick up life's pen and compose your living autobiography. Your storyline is your legacy; it will outlive you. (Note: *The greatest use of a life is to spend it on something that will outlast it. ~ William James)* Your life's story should be strategically and eloquently written. Cultivate your vision. Design your destiny. Your intentional decisions, coupled with your strategic actions will manifest your authentic life.

Cultivating Your Vision + Setting Your Intentions + Your Strategic Actions = Your Authentic Life ~ Dr. Keke

---

Chapter V: Elevated by Being Authentic
Self-Coaching Session

1. **What is your story?**

2. **Are you being your authentic self? How?**

3. **What is the vision for your life?**

4. **Who or what must you become, in order, to manifest your vision?**

5. **What is trying to emerge in your life?**

6. What do you need to eradicate from your life, in order, to gain clarity/a clear focus?

7. Have you ever pondered the question, "Who Am I?" Have you discovered who you truly are or are you still seeking your true identity? Please explain.

8. In what ways are you becoming/have become the person that you were created to be?

9. Do you have concerns about being your true self? Why or Why not? Please provide in-depth details.

10. Do you feel as if you must be secretive about your true intentions for various reasons? Please explain.

11. How have you been able to stand in your truth? Please share examples.

12. How has changing your thoughts or beliefs changed your life? Please be specific.

13. What do you perceive are your strongest characteristics?

14. How do you believe others truly feel about you? Provide an explanation.

15. Do you operate under a façade around certain individuals? Why or Why not?

16. What are you constantly being praised for?

17. What do others say are your bad habits?

18. How well do you listen and comprehend?

19. How can you communicate more effectively?

20. If you could take a year out of your life/a sabbatical to do anything that you would like, what would you do during this timeframe? Why? Identify at least (3) things that you would you put on your 'bucket list'. Please explain.

21. Identify at least (1) person in your life that you believe makes you better and explain why he/she is an asset to you.

22. If you had to choose only (1) word to adequately represent who you truly are, which adjective would you select that would accurately describe you? Why?

23. Please share how your past, good and bad, experiences are instrumental in cultivating your authenticity. Please provide a thorough response.

24. If you could change one choice that you have made in your life, what would it be? Do you believe that this decision hindered/altered the course of your life? How can you move forward to live the rest of your life unstuck and unstoppable?

25. What essential advice would you share with your younger self?

Chapter V: Elevated by Being Authentic
Self-Reflection Notes

_____

_____

_____

_____

_____

_____

_____

_____

_____

_____

_____

_____

_____

_____

IN CONCLUSION

Embarking upon my self-discovery journey, each day has been an amazing, purposeful awakening. I have found inner peace that transcends discord and confusion. The self-acceptance that I now embody has resulted in a serene sense of contentment.

Come to the realization that no matter what has occurred in your past, it doesn't have to define your future. You must put in the work to rewrite your story. *It is your life; it is your story.* It's never too late to begin anew. Do not be afraid to try. Failure is a learning curve. Delayed does not mean denied. You will win if you do not give up. You can *be*, *do*, and *have* whatever you desire. *You* are your best asset and advocate. You must believe in yourself. You are much smarter, braver, and stronger than you realize. You deserve the best; never settle for anything less than that.

Allow your experiences to elevate and catapult you towards greatness. Never become satisfied with being mediocre. Commit to mastery. In all that you do, strive for excellence. Design and live your life in such a way that you have no regrets. Operate at high-frequency levels and perform at your prime peak. When you set high standards, you will emit and attract what you expect from yourself and others.

Always be your true self. Get to know who you truly are. **You** should be one of the most fascinating and interesting people that you know. Become your own cheerleader. Nothing will ever give you as much confidence, satisfaction, and happiness as possessing the freedom to live out loud, stand in your truth, and fulfill your purpose.

In order to love who you are, you cannot hate the
experiences that shaped you. ~ Andrea Dykstra

You will become wiser and embolden from your past mistakes. My prayers for you are: that you will love and accept your true identity, be a light in this world, forgive yourself and others, be intentional and strategic about every decision that you make, live the highest expression of your very best self, use your divine gifts to empower others, design a path to your destiny, and be unapologetically authentic.

Be yourself. Everyone is already taken. ~ Oscar Wilde

My intention for writing *Elevated by Experiences* is to help you to recognize that you are powerful and invaluable. Begin or continue to genuinely love yourself as God loves you. Never doubt how incredible that you truly are. There is so much promise in you and the world needs the *authentic* you. You can do anything that you set your mind to. If you can dream it, you can do it. You do not need anyone to validate your skills, gifts, and talents. *It is your vision, not theirs.*

You can be your biggest enemy or your biggest cheerleader. Make the decision to only cultivate positive thoughts. The past is just that, the past. Stay focus only on what is in front of you. Be edified and elevated by your experiences. Always remember, that you owe it yourself to manifest your highest potential. You are an eagle; prepare to soar. I am praying for you.

Discomfort is inevitable whether you remain in a stagnant
story that no longer serves or you decide to choose
growth. So, choose growth. ~ Victoria Erickson

RECOMMENDED READING

If you want (1) year of prosperity, grow grain. If you want
(10) years of prosperity, grow trees. If you want (100)
years of prosperity, grow people. ~ Chinese Proverb

Holy Bible- <u>*THE*</u> *recommended textbook that is an invaluable resource that can help you navigate your way through life's lessons and exams. It is the curriculum and your study guide. Because you will be tested, the Lord's word will provide you with the knowledge that you need for sustainability. You are God's student and His pertinent instructions are vital for excelling this life's course. There are multiple Bible options, select the version that resonates with you.*

*Ambrosio, Sophia. #*Girl Boss*. New York, New York: Portfolio/Penguin, Putnam, 2014.

Bevere, Lisa. *Girls with Swords: How to Carry Your Cross Like a Hero.* Colorado Springs, Colorado: WaterBrook Press, 2014

Brown, Brene'. *Daring Greatly: How the Courage to Be Vulnerable Transforms the Way We Live, Love, Parent, and Lead.* New York: Avery/Penguin Random House, 2015

Burton, Valorie. *Successful Women Think Differently.* Eugene, Oregon: Harvest House Publishers, 2012.

Canfield, Jack. *The Success Principles: How to Get from Where You Are to Where You Want to Be.* New

York, New York: William Morrow/HarperCollins Publisher, 2005.

Clason, George S. *The Richest Man in Babylon*. New York: Hawthorn, 1955.

Coelho, Paulo. *The Alchemist*. New York: HarperCollins, 1998.

Covey, Stephen. *The 7 Habits of Highly Effective People: Powerful Lessons in Personal Change*. New York: Free Press, 1989

Duckworth, Angela. *Grit: The Power of Passion and Perseverance*. New York, NY: Scribner, 2016.

Duhigg, Charles. *The Power of Habit: Why We Do What We Do in Life and Business*. New York: Random House, 2012.

Dweck, Carol. *Mindset- The New Psychology of Success: How Can We Learn to Fulfill Our Potential*. New York: Random House, 2006.

Franklin, Devon. *Produced by Faith: Enjoy Real Success Without Losing Your True Self*. Nashville, Tennessee: Howard Books, 2011.

*Gilbert, Elizabeth. *Big Magic: Creative Living Beyond Fear*. New York: Riverhead Publishing/Penguin Group, 2015.

Greene, Robert. *48 Laws of Power*. New York City, NY: Viking Press/ Penguin Random House, 1998.

Harvey, Steve. *Act Like a Success, Think Like a Success: Discovering Your Gift and The Way to Life's Riches*. New York, New York: Amistad/ HarperCollins, 2014

Howes, Lewis. *The School of Greatness: A Real-World Guide to Living Bigger, Loving Deeper, and Leaving a Legacy*. New York, New York: Rodale, 2015

Jakes-Roberts, Sarah. *Lost and Found: Finding Hope in the Detours of Life*. Bloomingdale, Minnesota: Bethany House/Baker Publishing Group, 2014

Jakes, TD. *Destiny: Step into Your Purpose*. New York: FaithWords/ Hachette Book Group, 2015.

Jakes, TD. *Instinct: The Power to Unleash Your Inborn Drive*. New York: FaithWords/Hachette Book Group, 2014.

Nepo, Mark. *The Book of Awakening: Having the Life You Want by Being Present in the Life You Have*. New York: Penguin Group, 2012

O'Leary, John. *On Fire: The 7 Choices to Ignite a Radically Inspired Life*. New York, New York: North Star Way/Simon & Schuster, 2016

Pink, Daniel. *Drive: The Surprising Truth About What Motivates Us*. New York: Riverhead Books, 2009.

Robbins, Anthony. *Awaken the Giant Within*. New York: Free Press, 1991

Roberts, Touré. *Purpose Awakening: Discover the Epic Idea that Motivated Your Birth*. New York: FaithWords/Hachette Book Group, 2014.

Ruiz, Don Miguel. *The Four Agreements: A Practical Guide to Personal Freedom*. San Rafael, California: Amber-Allen Publishing, 1997

Sandberg, Sheryl. *Lean In: Women, Work, and The Will to Lead*. New York: Random House, 2013.

*Sincero, Jen. *You are a Bad Ass: How to Stop Doubting Your Greatness and Start Living an Awesome Life*. Philadelphia, Pennsylvania: Running Press, 2013.

Sinek, Simon. *Start with Why: How Great Leaders Inspire Everyone to Take Action*. New York, New York: Portfolio/Penguin Group, 2009.

Tolle, Eckhart. *A New Earth: Awakening to Your Life's Purpose.* Vancouver, BC: Namaste Publishing, 2004.

Tolle, Eckhart. *The Power of Now: A Guide to Spiritual Enlightenment.* Vancouver, BC: Namaste Publishing, 1997

Warren, Rick. *A Purpose Driven Life: What on Earth Am I Here For?* Grand Rapids, Michigan: Zondervan, 2002.

Zukav, Gary. *The Seat of the Soul.* New York, NY: Simon & Schuster, 1989.

Note: Some suggested readings may have strong and/or colorful language.

Don't compare your path with anybody else's.
Your path is unique to you. ~ Ram Dass

If this book was helpful to you in any capacity, please share it with someone else that you would like to encourage.

If you would like to share your story of how you've been elevated by your experiences, are following the path to your destiny, and/or creating your intentional and authentic life, I would love to hear from you.

Please write to me at
MyElevatedStory@gmail.com

Printed in the United States
By Bookmasters